T0025211

THE BEGINNER'S GUIDE TO

STOICISM

Tools for Emotional Resilience & Positivity

MATTHEW J. VAN NATTA

callisto
publishing
an imprint of Sourcebooks

INTRODUCTION

A decade ago, I discovered Stoicism and never stopped practicing. The Stoic way of thinking has reshaped my life and given me emotional resilience, a positive outlook, and the desire to change my community for the better. I've gained these benefits from my longtime practice. I learned how to build Stoic skills from a variety of books, an online community, and trial and error. It's my expectation that this guide will help you move forward at a quicker pace than I did, by providing a clear path upon which to travel.

I have lived with an anxiety disorder since my late teens. For too many years, it went untreated and wreaked havoc on my relationships and my professional life. In my early 30s, I sought out professional help and learned a variety of practices from Cognitive Behavioral Therapy (CBT) that worked and became constant tools in my mental life. Stoicism first drew me in because of the many similarities between the Stoic outlook and the therapy I had practiced. Later I would learn that there was a historical connection between the two. The difference was that CBT helped calm my thoughts, while Stoicism gave them direction. Stoicism helped me choose who I wanted to be and gave me the means to become that person. The process is ongoing, rewarding, and worth sharing.

Stoicism says you can thrive in life—no matter your circumstances. With this guide, you will learn to focus on the things you *can* control so your actions are impactful, and you aren't wasting your time on that which you can't change. You will become more open and accepting of others and, at the same time, have the courage to stand up for yourself and your beliefs. Your emotional life will benefit as you cultivate positivity and overcome negative thinking. You will become your best self and learn to live a life of harmony.

I have been an instructor for most of my adult life. When I took up Stoicism, it felt natural to share what I was learning. I began with my blog, *Immoderate Stoic*. I later created a podcast, *Good Fortune*, in homage to one of my favorite Marcus Aurelius quotes, "Here is the rule to remember in the future, When anything tempts you to be bitter: not, 'This is a misfortune' but 'To bear this worthily is good fortune.'" Both of these have been well received by the Stoic community and continue to help those who want to live a philosophical life. My teaching focuses on the practical. How can Stoicism help you right here, right now?

This guide is no different. You don't need a background in philosophy to benefit from its teachings. In the days when Stoicism developed, philosophy helped people live meaningful lives. The Stoic teachers provided an ethical basis for action in an often confusing and challenging world. Stoicism helps you get things done. You will learn to take control of your mental and emotional life. You will cultivate the skills needed to direct your actions in positive ways that help both you and everyone with whom you interact. If you are interested in gaining tools to sustain your happiness during all the ups and downs of life, you've come to the right place.

Stoicism trains you in a new way of thinking. I will lead you through this process step-by-step. Each chapter will build on the last. You will gain a firm foundation before you receive more information. Every chapter will also include practical lessons. You will get useful mental tools from the very beginning and, as you continue, their uses become even more apparent and powerful.

Part One: Foundations provides an overview of Stoicism as a philosophy and delves into its history. You will gain the context necessary to understand the goals of Stoic teaching. The framework of Stoicism will start to become clear.

Part Two: Your New Emotional Tool Kit lays the foundation of Stoic thought and practice. You will learn and use the three Stoic disciplines. You will look at virtue, the Stoic conception of personal excellence, so that your practice has a clear focus. You will also learn to separate the things you can control from those you cannot, a fundamental lesson that unlocks the true power of Stoicism.

Part Three: Stoicism for Life will take your new philosophical foundation and apply it to the day-to-day. You will learn to cultivate positive emotions and uproot the negative. Stoicism will make you more self-sufficient while it simultaneously motivates you to seek out healthy relationships with others. You'll also gain the courage to impact the world for the better.

It's time to start learning! First, you'll learn what Stoicism is—and what it definitely *isn't*. You'll learn a bit about its roots and how it has changed with the times. You'll also get introduced to the basic tools of the philosophy, which will help you cultivate a healthier mind and live out a more fulfilling life.

PART I

FOUNDATIONS

CHAPTER 1:
A Practical Philosophy

> *"To stop talking about what the good person is like, and just be one."*

—Marcus Aurelius, *Meditations* 10:16

How can you thrive in life? This book addresses that question. Here you will find a series of mental tools, daily mind-sets, guided practices, and more to help you be your best self in every moment, in any situation, for both your good and for the benefit of everyone around you. The philosophy behind these practices, Stoicism, has been helping a growing number of people overcome mental obstacles, become bold in the face of life's challenges, and find lasting satisfaction. In my own life,

Stoicism has helped me in large and small ways, from allowing me to manage a lifelong anxiety disorder to simply maintaining my peace during a long daily commute. I've also watched as this philosophy changed the lives of many others for the better. I know that Stoicism can help you find the means to flourish in this world, and I'm excited to share what it is all about.

What Is Stoicism?

A practical philosophy built on the belief that all people can lead flourishing lives, Stoicism maintains that the good life is available to you now, despite outer circumstances. However, you need to be willing to work toward cultivating a healthy mind. Stoicism teaches you to focus your thoughts and actions on that which you can control. In doing so, you'll develop a healthy mental outlook. Stoicism challenges you to evaluate both what you want and what you'd prefer to avoid. It teaches you to redirect your attention toward healthy desires and, as you do so, you'll find that positive emotions rise up more consistently. You'll gain emotional resilience, which will help you to overcome challenges to your happiness.

Above all, Stoicism aims to make you skillful at life. We call this life expertise *virtue*. The Stoic philosophy trains you in virtue: It sculpts your moral character into someone who is content, joyful, resilient, and able to take actions that make the world a better place.

MYTHS AND MISCONCEPTIONS

If you have never heard of Stoicism the philosophy, you have likely come across stoicism (small *s*) in your life. In modern English, the word *stoic* is used to describe people who remain self-possessed in the face of adversity. While often admirable, to be "stoic" has the potential to become unhealthy. If you merely repress emotions, holding back inner turmoil, but never truly deal with those internal issues, the outcome can be devastating. This is not Stoicism with a capital S. Even the ancient Stoics dealt with this mischaracterization of their philosophy; their critics saw it as a cold thing. And yet the Stoics insisted that no one should aim to be an unfeeling statue. Developing a virtuous life actually leads to a rich emotional life, one in which you are skillful with those emotions—cultivating the positive, while quickly overcoming the negative.

Another misconception is passivity. Stoicism says you can thrive in any situation; it teaches acceptance of the world as it is. This can be misinterpreted as apathy. "Why change," they say, "if one can be happy even in the worst of life's storms?"

It may seem paradoxical, but Stoic acceptance actually gives you the strength to overcome challenges. Passivity arises more often from fear than from acceptance. When a rude person makes aggressive demands, how often do you just give in, worrying that standing up for yourself would make matters worse? The Stoic accepts that the person in front of them is being hostile, but they can choose how to respond. If the belligerent person's demands are unjust, the Stoic works for justice. Stoicism teaches you to be clear-eyed so you can make the best possible choices. As you learn to trust your capacity to tackle trials, inaction and indecision stop being obstacles. When you direct your attention toward what you can control, your actions become well-aimed and effective.

Before we look in depth at the tools Stoicism provides, let's look briefly at where these ideas began.

ORIGINS

Stoicism began in ancient Greece in 300 BCE, flourished for 500 years, but then faded away, seen only in fits and starts throughout the years until the rather recent resurgence of which you are now a part. The founder of the philosophy was Zeno of Citium, a merchant who lost everything in a shipwreck. After this loss, he turned to philosophy to rebuild his life. Zeno came to believe that all people were meant to have a "good flow of life," one that consisted of personal serenity while also moving in joyful harmony with their community. To reach people with his message, Zeno taught public lessons outdoors. He and his students would meet in a *stoa*, a covered walkway common in his time. His school became known as the Stoa, which is where we get the name Stoicism.

As time moved on, Stoicism would find its way to the Roman empire, or rather the Roman Empire would find its way to Greece. It's with the Roman Stoics that we'll spend much of our time. This is because the works of the Greek Stoics are nearly completely lost to us. We know that they wrote thousands of books, but we're left with only pages. From the Roman Stoics, the works of three men in particular have made it to us relatively intact, saving the wisdom of their philosophy from extinction:

- **Epictetus (50–135 CE), a Stoic teacher who began life as a slave and gives us the most complete example of the philosophy's teachings;**

- **The Roman senator Seneca (4 BCE–65 CE), who provides us with illuminating insights;**

- **Marcus Aurelius (121–180 CE), though emperor of Rome, will be most like our peer in this journey. We** have access to his personal philosophical journal, and it allows us access to the inner thoughts of a practicing Stoic.

BC, BCE, AND CE

BCE (Before the Common Era) and CE (Common Era) will be used in this book whenever you see dates. This is the accepted convention throughout most academic disciplines. If you are used to BC/AD notations, fear not: BCE exactly replaces BC, and CE is the same as AD.

MODERN STOICISM

> *"I do not bind myself to some particular one of the Stoic teachers. I too have a right to form an opinion."*
>
> —Seneca, *On the Happy Life*

Modern Stoicism focuses heavily on ethics. The ancient Stoics divided their schooling into three broad topics: physics, logic, and ethics. While there is intellectual value in reading Stoic thoughts on physics and logic, most Stoics want to get to the part that helps them thrive. The Stoic approach to living has captured our attention. In fact, a modern therapeutic practice, Cognitive Behavioral Therapy (CBT), was influenced by Stoic writings. Much of its approach to emotional life and many of its practices align with Stoicism. CBT helps people think in a healthier way but does not provide a road map to a flourishing life. The Stoic philosophy uses similar mental practices but combines them with a set of values that can guide you toward your best self. It's that coupling of mental clarity with a sense of purpose that has attracted so many to Stoicism.

Modern Stoicism also looks at our relationship with the universe differently. Many ancient Stoics were pious pantheists who perceived the universe as a benevolent god known as Zeus. Modern practice embraces a more secular point of view. If you are not religious, Stoicism retains all its usefulness. If you are religious and choose to adopt Stoicism, the philosophy meshes better if its theology is left behind.

ABOUT PANTHEISTS

People often refer to the ancient Stoics as pantheists. This is a bit anachronistic, as pantheism is a modern conception—the term itself didn't arise until 1697 CE. That said, Stoic theology does fit the pantheist definition of either believing that god is the universe or that the universe is a manifestation of god.

Most early Stoics believed that the entire universe was interconnected as one being, a single organism they called Zeus, who is synonymous with Nature and Reason. The Roman historian Diogenes Laertius tells us, "[The Stoics] also say that God is an animal, immortal, rational, perfect in happiness, immune to all evil, providentially taking care of the world and of all that is in the world, but he is not of human shape. He is the creator of the universe, and as it were, the Father of all things in common, and that a part of him pervades everything, which is called by different names, according to its powers . . ."

In modern times, Stoic practice is more personalized than in the past. It's unlikely that you will live at a Stoic school like Epictetus's students did. This doesn't mean you have to be lonely! There are vibrant online communities dedicated to Stoicism and a growing number of groups all over the world who meet face-to-face to discuss the philosophy. There are even conferences for practical Stoicism. If you head to Modernstoicism.com, you can learn about Stoicon, a yearly gathering for both practitioners and the philosophically curious. Stoicon coincides with Stoic Week, an event dedicated to promoting human well-being through the Stoic philosophy. I aim to leave you with a solid foundation so you can thrive on your own, but there's a growing world out there for you to participate in.

Stoicism is here for anyone: It says that all human beings are family and each of us are worthy of a loving respect. Stoicism proclaims that all people are capable of living lives of wisdom. Even in ancient times the philosophy reached a diverse range of people. As already mentioned, the Stoic teacher Epictetus began life as a slave, while the practitioner Marcus Aurelius led an empire; Stoicism has been inclusive since its origin. Although it developed in societies that were highly patriarchal, Stoic writings clearly put forth that women are moral equals who deserve to be trained in philosophy. Even so, among the old Stoics we primarily find men—often affluent ones—and they were sometimes locked into the thinking of their times. Thankfully we are not bound by Greek and Roman customs. Our modern community lives up to the best of Stoic thought and contains a diverse, vibrant, and growing population.

REFLECTION

When you are ready to begin some undertaking, remind yourself what the nature of that undertaking is. If you are going out of the house to bathe, put before your mind what happens at a public bath—those who splash you with water, those who jostle against you, those who vilify you and rob you. You will set about your undertaking more securely if before beginning you say to yourself, "I want to take a bath, and, at the same time, to keep my moral purpose in harmony with nature." And do this for every undertaking. For if anything happens to hinder you in your bathing, you will be ready to say, "Oh, well, this was not the only thing that I wanted, but I wanted also to keep my moral purpose in harmony with nature; and I will not do that if I am annoyed at what is going on."

—EPICTETUS, *ENCHIRIDION* 4

Continuous Stoic practice reshapes your moral character. The fundamental focus of Stoicism involves that character—your best self—because this is wholly within your control. The next time you do anything, remind yourself: "I want to do this task, and, at the same time, I want to protect my harmony."

Ask yourself:

- In the task before me, what challenges could arise?

- In confronting those challenges, how can I be my best self and remain in harmony with life?

WHY STOICISM?

You have the capacity to thrive. The Stoic goal is *eudaimonia*, a flourishing life. With focused practice, you can cultivate a life that's serene, joyful, and enthusiastic, even in the face of great challenges. You will find yourself less angry, anxious, and lonely as your Stoic mind-set makes negative emotions less likely to take root.

I work as a health and safety instructor. Each morning, I drive to a different business in Oregon to train a group of people I've never met. My morning commute can range from 15 minutes to three hours. The groups I meet might be attentive and inquisitive or they may be sneaking looks at their phones or obviously frustrated that they have to attend my training. On top of this, there may be personal issues in my own life that could distract me from giving my best presentation. I begin my day with a Stoic meditation that reminds me I am capable of facing any obstacle I meet. I have mental tools like the *Dichotomy of Control*, which helps me focus on those things I have the ability to change. Stoicism has given me the *Festival Mind-set*, in which every crowd becomes a party and which helps me enjoy what others may find frustrating. At night, I do an *Evening Review*, which allows me to openly evaluate myself and leads me to improve myself day by day. Soon, you will have these same tools and much more. With practice, you'll gain the flourishing life that Stoicism promises.

Before we move forward, take a moment to think about how I've described the Stoic life. It's:

- **flourishing**

- **in good flow**

- **in harmony with nature**

Right now, what do these phrases mean to you? If you were to attain the goal of living a flourishing life in harmony with nature, what would that look like? What steps could you take today to bring yourself closer to this vision?

STOICISM FOR EVERYONE

How you define a "good flow of life" is unique to you. The challenges you face in life are likely wildly different from my challenges. Thankfully, each of us can apply the tools of Stoicism for our own particular purposes. For example, I watched my wife use the philosophy during a difficult pregnancy. Doctors cautioned us throughout that time that our daughter may not survive and that Christy's life was at risk as well. Despite an uncertain future, she focused on the present, which let her find joy in the moment. She placed her attention on her thoughts and opinions, the things she controlled, which kept her from being overwhelmed by life's anxieties. The Stoic mind-set provided peace amid turmoil. Practitioners use the philosophy to show up fully in relationships, to find fulfillment in work (often *in spite of* that work), and to manage day-to-day struggles. I've also met Stoics who use the philosophy to manage addiction, chronic pain, or, like myself, emotional issues. Whatever challenges will come your way, Stoicism provides a means of thriving as you face them.

In order to access all these benefits, you will need to look at yourself clearly, be open to exploring the unique perspective that Stoicism offers, and be willing to practice diligently. As Musonius Rufus, a Roman Stoic teacher, said, "Practicing each virtue always must follow learning the lessons appropriate to it, or it is pointless for us to learn about it." Accepting this, let's take a look at the many tools at your disposal.

IN THE MOMENT

Take a moment to recall a situation in which you felt content or joyful.

- **What aspects of that moment do you think most contributed to your happiness?**

- **What mind-set allowed you to experience those positive emotions?**

- **How might you access that mind-set in any circumstance, not just that particular moment?**

The Tool Kit

Of all the Stoic tools you will receive, the Dichotomy of Control is the most fundamental. Its premise: Some things are in your control, and some things are outside of your control. Stoics divide every situation according to this and focus only on the former. This simple practice represents the core of a Stoic's orientation to the world. It helps you decide where to place your attention so your actions are effective. Every practice, meditation, and action begins by training your attention on that which you can control.

Stoic training centers around three disciplines and four virtues.

- **The disciplines provide the training needed to develop a Stoic outlook.**

- **The virtues give a definition of excellence, so you have a vision to work toward.**

The three disciplines seem to have been developed by Epictetus both to inform Stoic practice and to act as a structure for his school's curriculum. We know that it was influential enough to have impacted Marcus Aurelius; he clearly references this threefold perspective throughout his writing.

The Stoics inherited the four virtues from a longer tradition that extends at least as far back as Plato and Socrates, although it's quite likely that this structure is even older.

DISCIPLINES

Here's a brief overview of the three Stoic disciplines, which we'll look at in detail in chapter 3 (page 40).

- *The Discipline of Desire* entails a radical realignment of your values as you work to desire only what is within your complete control. Redirecting your attention in this way will free you from chasing after things that do not contribute to your happiness.

- *The Discipline of Action* relates to your interactions with other people. The aim is to seek healthy, positive relationships with everyone you meet, even knowing others may not reciprocate.

- *The Discipline of Assent* concerns your thoughts about life. You learn to separate your initial reactions to the world from your final judgments about the world. You refuse to walk down mental paths that lead to negativity, instead evaluating your thoughts in order to align with wisdom.

Within each of the disciplines you find a variety of techniques that help you cultivate a healthy mental life.

Consider this: How would it feel to have a consistently positive mental outlook?

VIRTUES

Virtue is the art of living in harmony with the world. Stoicism sees you as just as much a part of nature as any other thing. It says that you can learn to interact with the world in a way that best expresses your natural humanity and your unique self. In this way, the purpose of Stoicism is to develop into your best self. The ancient Stoics tended to use four primary virtues as guides for thoughts and actions, which I refer to as:

- **Wisdom**

- **Courage**

- **Justice**

- **Moderation**

These are not all of the named virtues. Justice, for instance, is often broken down into the subcategories of kindness and fairness.

Here's one way to think of it: If you send white light through a prism, all of the colors become distinct—but they come from the same light. Similarly, your virtue is unified, but it can be viewed more distinctly through the facet of life you're encountering. For example, Wisdom is virtue applied to your thought process. Courage is virtue applied to your emotional life. Justice is virtue in relationship with other people. Moderation is virtue as applied to our choices. Every situation presents an opportunity to practice virtue. When I notice someone else could benefit from my seat on the bus, do I get up? When I have a chance to honestly discuss a difficulty with a coworker, do I take it? Choosing to act with virtue will allow you to thrive and live in harmony.

A core belief that separates Stoic thought from most other ancient philosophies—and modern ones—is that virtue is the *only* good. Stoics claim that only virtue is good in all circumstances. Justice is always good. Wisdom is never bad. The things many consider "good"—money, fame, and even health—can work to your benefit, no doubt, but can also play out in damaging ways. Stoicism challenges you to focus on virtue, because when you are your best self you will use the stuff of life in the best way.

Consider this: What would you say is the greatest good in life?

Rules to Live By

Remember: Your mind is yours—and yours alone. If you focus on healthy thoughts and develop balanced opinions about your situation, you will cultivate positive emotions and find lasting enthusiasm to live your best life. You will see negativity for what it is: a waste of energy. You will learn to stop allowing fear, anger, and other anxieties to grow. You will discover not only that you can weather challenges, but you often find them enjoyable. As you move in this direction, the work of being yourself will become a joy. To gain all of this, you simply need the right tools and the will to use them. Let's begin.

TIME LINE OF STOIC THINKERS

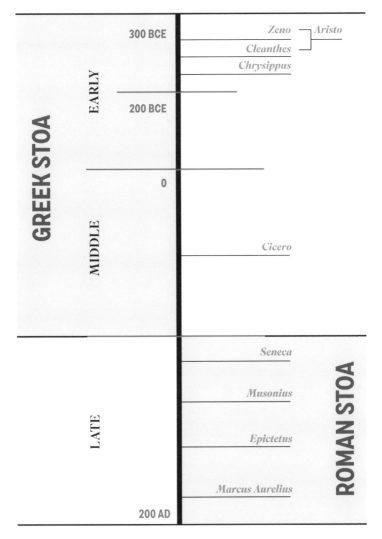

GREEK STOA

EARLY

300 BCE

200 BCE

Zeno — *Aristo*
Cleanthes
Chrysippus

MIDDLE

0

Cicero

ROMAN STOA

LATE

Seneca

Musonius

Epictetus

Marcus Aurelius

200 AD

CHAPTER 2:
A Quick Trip Through History

"Zeno used then to discourse, pacing up and down in the painted colonnade or stoa . . . people came henceforth to hear him, and this is why they were known as men of the Stoa, or Stoics; and the same name was given to his followers, who had formerly been known as Zenonians."

—Diogenes Laertius, *Lives of the Eminent Philosophers*, Book 7

S toicism originates from ancient Greeks in 300 BCE, but the philosophy we now know filtered through later Romans. Looking into the lives of the people who developed the philosophy can help us appreciate it in new ways. Stoics were real people, the same as us. If they could create and practice a philosophy of human flourishing, we can as well. Let's meet some of the people behind it!

Before Stoicism

Before Zeno of Citium developed the philosophy that became Stoicism, he studied quite a few philosophies. His first influence came from the Cynic teacher, Crates. One of the Cynics' core tenets will sound familiar: The purpose of life is to live in virtue. Cynics practiced virtue by rejecting more conventional desires. Zeno also studied Platonism under Xenocrates and Polemon. Like Plato's followers, Zeno held Socrates up as an exemplary human. The Stoics considered themselves direct philosophical descendants of Socrates. Zeno also studied the Megarians, who may have influenced his belief in the unity of virtue. From these rich influences and more, Zeno developed something new, a philosophy that thrived for 500 years and has never fully left us.

First Philosophers

The people whose influence on Stoicism lives on today include the following, listed chronologically from the earliest to the most recent.

■ **ZENO (CIRCA 334–262 BCE)**

"Happiness is a good flow of life."

—Zeno, as quoted by Stobaeus

What we know of Zeno of Citium, the founder of Stoicism, comes from a biography by ancient historian Diogenes Laertius. One story about his younger life says, "He consulted the oracle to know what he should do to attain the best life, and that the god's response was that he should take on the complexion of the dead." Zeno decided this meant he should study ancient writers, and it's through this that his love of philosophy blossomed.

According to Diogenes Laertius, Zeno was a merchant sailing with his goods when a storm left him shipwrecked. Unsure what to do in life, Zeno made his way to Athens, went to a bookseller, and read an account of Socrates' life. Impressed by what he learned, Zeno asked the bookseller where he could find people like Socrates. At that moment, a famous Cynic philosopher, Crates of Thebes, passed by. The bookseller pointed and said, "Follow him."

We may not know exactly how it happened, but we know Zeno arrived in Athens around 312 BCE and that by 300 BCE he started the Stoic school. His own philosophy retained the threefold division of logic, physics, and ethics from his Platonist days, though his physics differed significantly from that of Plato. His ethics retained much from the Cynics, though the Stoics were less dramatic in their asceticism.

Zeno wrote many books, but today we only have titles. Early Stoic works were lost to philosophical purges where books were burned, to general neglect, and to the ravages of time. What we know of Zeno comes in glimpses from quotes and other fragments. We know that Zeno wrote *The Republic*, a book that described a perfect Stoic world. Zeno made bold claims for his time: He insisted that all people should be seen as equal citizens, which included equality among men and women. Zeno believed that all people had equal access to virtue, but few ever perfected it. Socrates, Diogenes, and the mythic Hercules were some of the few people he held up as *sages*, the truly virtuous. This might be why the early name, Zenonians, never stuck: Zeno never claimed to be perfect. Instead, the school was named for the place it was taught—the Stoa—where lessons were open to anyone.

■ ARISTO OF CHIOS (CIRCA 300–CIRCA 260 BCE)

"Virtue is the health of the soul."

—Aristo

Aristo was a contemporary of Zeno. His philosophy shows the wide divergence of Stoic thought from its origins. Aristo believed that only ethics mattered. His views did not prevail, as Zeno's ideas were solidified by the third head of the Stoic school, Chrysippus, and became

Stoicism proper. Even though Aristo seemingly lost that ancient battle, I find that his choice to drop logic and physics to emphasize practical ethics fits with our modern spirit.

▪ CLEANTHES (CIRCA 330–CIRCA 230 BCE)

After he died, Zeno bequeathed his school to one of his students, Cleanthes. Cleanthes began life as a boxer but switched careers to become a philosopher after hearing Zeno's lectures. Cleanthes valued physical labor and supported himself both as a student and later as the second head of the school through hard toil. He worked nights as a water carrier for a gardener, irrigating the land by walking from the well to the garden and back again. Cleanthes kept the Stoa for over 30 years, expanding and solidifying a variety of Zeno's doctrines. Zeno told his pupils to "live consistently." Cleanthes added, "with nature." He supposedly wrote more than 50 works, but again, we only have fragments. One of the longest works that we still have is called "Hymn to Zeus," which gives us an idea of the Stoic relationship with their god, the universe. This prayer was just a part of his hymn:

"To wherever your decrees have assigned me.

I follow readily, but if I choose not,

Wretched though I am, I must follow still.

Fate guides the willing, but drags

the unwilling."

■ CHRYSIPPUS (CIRCA 279–CIRCA 206 BCE)

Chrysippus was Cleanthes's student and the third head of the Stoic school. We know that he was a brilliant philosopher and that he greatly expanded on Zeno's teachings, so much so that he is called the Second Founder of Stoicism. Diogenes Laertius said, "Without Chrysippus, there would be no Stoa."

■ CICERO (106–43 BCE)

In 155 BCE, the head of the Stoic school, accompanied by other philosophers, went to Rome. They made such a strong impression that in the mid-40s BCE a famous Roman statesman and orator, Cicero, wrote multiple books about Stoic ideas. He did not consider himself a Stoic, citing differences with their physics and other ideas, but he practiced Stoic ethics, and his works pass on information that otherwise would have been lost.

■ SENECA (4 BCE–65 CE)

Seneca was also a Roman statesman who famously advised Emperor Nero in the early years of Nero's reign. Seneca was a practicing Stoic and, as a prolific writer, wrote 124 letters on morality and a variety of essays that constitute one of the more important bodies of Stoic thought to which we still have access.

■ MUSONIUS RUFUS (CIRCA 30–100 CE)

Musonius Rufus was the teacher of a better-known Stoic, Epictetus. We have a small collection of his lectures, which illuminate Stoic thoughts on a range of subjects, such as what Stoics should eat, how they should dress and furnish their homes, and their relationship to work and family. Epictetus states that his teacher did not want students to praise his words, but to be stunned into contemplative silence. As Musonius said, "The philosopher's school is a doctor's office. You must leave not pleased, but pained."

■ EPICTETUS (55–135 CE)

We know of Epictetus because a student, Arrian, transcribed his lectures in the *Discourses* and the *Enchiridion*. Epictetus started life as a slave, was given his freedom, and became a Stoic teacher. His influence on modern Stoicism is hard to overestimate: He likely developed the three Disciplines. A true Stoic, Epictetus always focused on changing the lives of his students. He didn't want them to mistake memorization of Stoic texts for the real work of building a better self. "If you are acting in harmony, show me that," he said, "and I will tell you that you are making progress; but if out of harmony, begone, and do not confine yourself to expounding your books, heck, go and write some books yourself. And what will you gain?"

◼ MARCUS AURELIUS (121 CE–180 CE)

"Not to feel exasperated or defeated or despondent because your days aren't packed with wise and moral actions. But to get back up when you fail, to celebrate behaving like a human—however imperfectly—and fully embrace the pursuit you've embarked on." –Marcus Aurelius, *Meditations* 5:9

From 161 to 180 CE, Roman emperor Marcus Aurelius kept a personal philosophical journal. That journal, now often titled *Meditations*, is one of the primary surviving Stoic works. It's through his musings that we understand the Stoic mind. His thoughts are wide ranging, but we find someone who wrestles with his own thoughts, seeks practical wisdom, and, as emperor, yearns to understand justice. He also contemplates his life in light of the universe's immensity in both space and time. Marcus shows us that no matter a person's social standing, they can find Stoic harmony.

Know Your Stoics

Let's see if you can recall the lives of the Stoics. Match the life fact with the philosopher it represents.

ZENO OF CITIUM   A. started out as a slave, but was granted his freedom and became head of the Stoic school

CLEANTHES   B. a Roman statesman whose letters on morality form a large part of the Stoic writings that remain

CHRYSIPPUS   C. a shipwrecked merchant who changed course and became a philosopher

SENECA   D. a brilliant philosopher who has been called "the second founder of Stoicism"

EPICTETUS   E. the emperor of Rome who wrote a personal philosophical journal we still have today

MARCUS AURELIUS   F. a boxer in his youth who worked long hours to support his Stoic teaching

Answer key page 165

Even More Philosophers!

These famous thinkers predate the Stoics yet all influenced Stoic philosophy in one significant way or another.

■ PYTHAGORAS (570–495 BCE)

If you remember your math, you'll recall the Pythagorean Theorem. If your math instructor tried to make things interesting, you may have learned that Pythagoras the mathematician was also a religious leader. His political and religious thoughts were highly influential in ancient Greece and inspired many philosophers. Many Stoic texts reference Pythagoras and his Golden Sayings. The Stoics particularly enjoyed a Pythagorean practice that asks you to review your day by asking, "What have I done wrong? What have I done well? What have I left that must be done tomorrow?"

■ SOCRATES (470–399 BCE)

Everyone knows Socrates as the founder of Western philosophy. The Stoics traced their own history directly to this enigmatic man and model philosopher, though their school developed almost a hundred years after his death. The life of Socrates inspired Zeno of Citium to become a philosopher. What we know of Socrates comes only from others' writings; he chose not to write at all but to live a life of philosophical dialogue with pretty much everyone he ever met. Many of Socrates's views—that no one desires to do evil, that no one makes a mistake willingly, and that virtue is sufficient for happiness—were adopted into Stoicism.

■ DIOGENES OF SINOPE (CIRCA 412–323 BCE)

"And how is it possible that a man who has nothing, who is naked, houseless, without a hearth, squalid, without a servant, without a city, can live a life that flows easily? See, God has sent you a man to show you that it is possible."

—Epictetus, concerning Diogenes of Sinope

Diogenes of Sinope founded Cynic philosophy and, like Socrates, was held by later Stoics as a supreme example of the philosophical life. Cynicism involves more ascetic practice than Stoicism. Many Cynics choose to own only the clothes on their back, and they challenged their bodies to show that they were above discomfort. Diogenes of Sinope himself slept in a large ceramic jar that he found in a marketplace. The Cynic idea that everything but virtue is completely indifferent led to this intentional poverty and defiance of social norms. After all, if things are neither good nor bad in themselves, then why invest in them? The Stoics would adopt much of this view but add the idea that there are things that are worth obtaining, all things considered. Diogenes of Sinope inspired the Stoics with his willingness to fully embody his beliefs and challenge society in pursuit of wisdom.

MODERN CYNICISM VS. ANCIENT CYNICISM

The term "cynic" (or "cynicism") probably evokes the modern sense of the word, meaning a person who is self-interested, distrustful, and willing to disregard social norms in order to get ahead. This view of cynicism is as far removed from the ancient Cynic philosophy as the modern word "stoic" is distant from the ancient Stoics. The Cynics believed that the purpose of life was to live a life of virtue, like the Stoics, but their practice was to discard as many material things as possible in order to live that life. They also disregarded most social conventions, not out of self-interest, but because they regarded them as obstacles to the virtuous life and felt their scandalous behavior provided an opportunity for others to learn to question the world around them.

Greek Lesson

Knowing these terms commonly used by the Stoics helps give a greater understanding of their school of thought.

Eudaimonia [ew-die-mo-NEE-ah], noun: Happiness, human flourishing.
The Stoics consider human flourishing the point of life. They define this as, "Living according to nature."

Prosoche [pro-soh-KHAY], noun: Attention.
A fundamental aspect of Stoic practice is a focused attention on your thought process.

Pathos [PEY-thos], noun: An unreasonable judgment; a disturbance of the mind.
The Stoics believed that negative emotions occur because of improper judgments about the world. Stoic ethical practices retrain us to make reasoned judgment and therefore eliminate pathos, which are also called passions.

Eupatheiai [ew-pa-THAY-eye], noun: A reasonable judgment; a healthy state of mind.
Healthy states of mind, such as joy, come from reasonable beliefs about—and reactions to—the world.

Arete [ar-eh-TAY], noun: Virtue, excellence.
Training yourself to strive for personal moral excellence will allow you to access eudaimonia, the flourishing life.

Adiaphora [ah-die-ah-FO-rah], noun: Indifferents.
The Stoics put all things that are outside of your control into the category of "indifferents," things that, in themselves, are neither good nor bad. A key part of Stoic training is learning to discern between truly good things and indifferents.

Oikeiosis [oy-KAY-o-sees], noun: Affinity, affiliation, endearment.
Stoicism works on our natural affection for close relatives in order to expand it to include love for all humankind.

Applying the Theory

Let's use Pythagoras's technique to review *your* most recent past: yesterday. Ideally, practice this every night, just before going to sleep. First, look back on your day: What do you feel was unsuccessful? What did you do well? Finally, is there anything that you left undone that could be addressed tomorrow? Celebrate your triumphs. Use lessons from your mistakes to make progress tomorrow.

The Stoics you just met created a practical philosophy that can help you to thrive. In the next two chapters, you will work with the tools that they used to conquer challenges and to find harmony in their lives. The Stoic disciplines will provide a structure for understanding Stoicism, and the virtues will give direction to your philosophical work.

PART II

YOUR NEW EMOTIONAL TOOL KIT

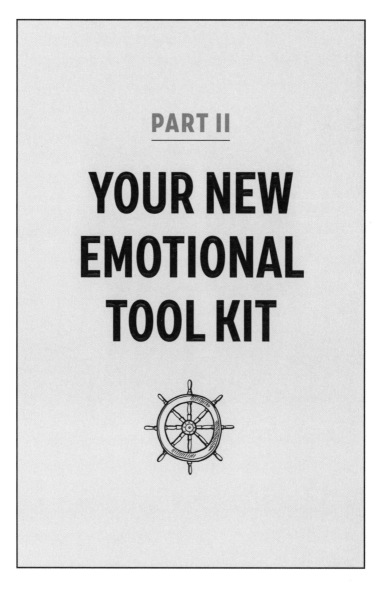

CHAPTER 3

Thinking Like a Stoic

> *"Everywhere, at each moment, you have the option, to accept this event with humility, to treat this person as he should be treated, to approach this thought with care, so that nothing irrational creeps in."*

—Marcus Aurelius, *Meditations* 7:54

Think Stoically

Stoicism gives you the tools to thrive in life by working with your mind. If you have a healthy mental life, then you can find positivity and resilience in any situation. The quote that opens this chapter addresses all three of the Stoic disciplines. The

Discipline of Desire will help you accept events with humility. New values will free you to practice moderation and help you find courage when facing life events. The Discipline of Action will help you develop a love of justice and treat people as they should be treated. The Discipline of Assent will give you a rational perspective to approach every thought with care.

An exercise program for your brain, the disciplines train your mind so that you can live a life that maximizes happiness. The Stoic mind-set is unshakable. This mind-set doesn't develop by shrinking from the world, but by engaging with your community in a reasonable and affectionate way. After all, your goal is to live in harmony, and harmony involves other people. After you learn about the disciplines, which give structure to Stoicism, you will learn about the virtues—the disciplines show you what to do, and the virtues show you the why.

Essential Tools

The disciplines, paired with the virtues, will help you cultivate a healthy mind-set that allows you to be your best self in every situation. You'll be able to cultivate a positive and resilient emotional life that allows for more consistent access to serenity and joy. Think of them as a framework upon which you hang your Stoic thoughts.

THE DISCIPLINE OF DESIRE: WANTING WHAT YOU HAVE

> *"As long as you do what's proper to your nature, and accept what the world's nature has in store—as long as you work for others' good, by any and all means—what is there that can harm you?"*
>
> —Marcus Aurelius, *Meditations* 11:13

Epictetus believed the Discipline of Desire was the most important practice for a new Stoic. He advised his pupils to focus on this area because future advancement in Stoicism required the healthy mind-set that would emerge from practicing this discipline. Desire is an expansion of your mind toward something you want; the opposite of aversion (or fear), which is a contraction from something.

Epictetus explained the point of controlling desire and aversion with a simple truth: If you never get what you want, you will never be happy, and if you run into what you've been trying to avoid, you will lose whatever happiness you have. To develop consistent happiness, you must train yourself to desire only what you can always have, and fear only what you can always avoid. The Discipline of Desire exists to give you this mind-set, one that remains undisturbed by life's challenges.

For example, picture passengers on a plane during turbulence. They are all having a similar physical experience, but there's a range of mental states: The man in the window seat is overwhelmed by fear, the woman in the middle seat is perfectly calm, and the person near the aisle is asleep. They're experiencing the same thing physically—the feeling of turbulence—but they have different outlooks. The fearful person focuses on frightening thoughts, worrying about a possible plane crash. The calm woman uses her mind differently. If she is a Stoic, maybe she's reminding herself that she doesn't know the future and she can't control the turbulence. She may understand that panicking does nothing to keep the plane in the sky, but knows worry could incapacitate her, making her less useful to herself and to others should the situation escalate. Two people in two very different emotional states. Which would you rather be?

The Stoic mind-set involves understanding what you can control and what you cannot. You ask yourself—what desires can I always obtain, and what things can I always avoid? The

Stoic answer is if you only desire to be your best (to live with virtue) and if you only avoid moral mistakes (called vice), then you can always succeed because these are things that you control.

To manage both your desires and aversions, you must focus on the present. The things we control are here, in this moment. As Seneca put it, "These two things must be cut away: fear of the future, and the memory of past sufferings. The latter no longer concerns me, and the future does not concern me yet." So many of our desires and fears exist out there in the future and yet they find a way to bother us through our present thoughts. Soon, you will practice "fencing off" the present so you can concentrate your energy on the here and now. (See Circle the Present, page 45.)

Disciplining desire also means learning to accept the present moment. If you want to act powerfully in the moment, you must react to what lies in front of you. Wishing things were different is a waste of energy. The term *amor fati*, the love of fate, comes from the more modern philosopher Nietzsche. The idea, however, runs throughout the Stoic philosophy. If you can accept the world as it is, you will not desire things that will never be. This is not meant to discourage you from striving for better; after all, how would you have the virtue Courage if that were the case? But if you can't come to terms with what is happening before you, your happiness will always be interrupted.

Placing your personal life into a larger context, even a universal one, can help curb negative thinking by putting your challenges into perspective. The Stoics practiced a variety of techniques to adopt a universal perspective, one of which you will practice in just a moment. First, let's look at a variety of practices that come from the Discipline of Desire.

Circle the Present

> *"Then remind yourself that past and future have no power over you. Only the present—and even that can be minimized. Just mark off its limits."*

—Marcus Aurelius, *Meditations* 8:36

"Mark off its limits," references a practice called *circling the present*. It provides a way to relieve stress, catastrophic thinking, and other anxieties. To do this, you only allow yourself to dwell on the present, essentially fencing yourself off from the future and the past. Take a breath. Draw your attention to the present moment. The past is finished. The future is unknowable. Leave anxieties about the future alone; they solely exist in your imagination. You can only act in the present.

- **Can you handle this moment?**

- **What can you do right now to have healthy thoughts and to take helpful actions?**

Infinite Opportunity

When your desires and aversions are things or situations, you will think of moments that don't provide what you want or moments that confront you with things you'd avoid as "bad." If you stop focusing on outcomes—but instead desire being your best at every moment—you'll understand that every situation provides an opportunity to practice virtue.

When confronted by a challenge, ask yourself:

- **How can I benefit from this?**

- **What virtue can I draw on to meet this moment?**

Pause and Compare

> *"If you have received an impression of any pleasure, guard yourself and create a delay. Then think of the time you will enjoy the pleasure, and the time after, when you will repent and be disappointed with yourself. On the other side, imagine your happiness if you resist the temptation and get to commend yourself for the victory."*

—Epictetus, *Enchiridion* 34

We all have pleasures that, for us, are unhealthy. It can be hard to overcome your desire in the moment. Sometimes, you can simply avoid the situation in question, so you aren't tempted, but the Stoics always remind you that you can't leave your happiness to chance. You will encounter instances where you need to make a decision. This is when you *pause and compare.* Step 1 is to find a way to delay your choice. Can you leave the area for a moment? Can you pause and take a breath? Give yourself time to think. Next, compare two possibilities: choosing the pleasure versus choosing excellence (virtue). Remember that the pleasure includes both the moment you do it *and* your feelings about yourself after the fact. This practice will help you overcome initial impulses and make a more reasoned choice.

The View from Above

Sit in a comfortable place, close your eyes, and picture yourself from above. As you look at yourself, pull back, and see your neighborhood. Then your town, your country, the world, perhaps even the universe. As you do this, at each stage, put your challenges in relationship to what you are seeing. Notice that others are also confronting challenges. Understand that the world isn't so focused on you that your mistakes are seen by all. Allow your troubles to fade into the distance for this moment. Find peace in the world and in your small part of it.

- Is there anything in your life that you used to really want or fear, that you no longer do?

- Why did that change?

REFLECTION

"Don't panic before the picture of your entire life. Don't dwell on all the troubles you've faced or have yet to face, but instead ask yourself as each trouble comes: What is so unbearable or unmanageable in this? Your reply will embarrass you. Then remind yourself that it's not the future or the past that bears down on you, but only the present. Always the present, which becomes an even smaller thing when isolated in this way and when the mind that cannot bear up under so slender an object is chastened."

—MARCUS AURELIUS, *MEDITATIONS* 8:36

This quote directly illustrates *circling the present*. Recall a time when you were very worried about an event, but after it was over, you realized the worry was overblown. Use this event as your practice. Imagine having lived through it while employing this technique.

- How would things have changed if your energy was in the present instead of lost in thought of the future?

THE DISCIPLINE OF ACTION: WHAT YOU DO

> *"Impassivity with regard to the events, brought about by an exterior cause. Justice in the actions brought about by the cause that is within you. In other words, let your impulse to act and your action have as their goal the service of the human community, because that, for you, is in conformity with your nature."*
>
> —Marcus Aurelius, *Meditations* 9:31

We have to make decisions and take some risks in this life, but taking action doesn't guarantee you get what you want. How can you be in harmony if failure is an option? The Discipline of Action is focused on the virtue Justice, which we will explore further in the next chapter. For now, know that this discipline asks three things of you:

- First, learn to take actions with a "reserve clause" (more on this soon).

- Second, learn to choose actions that benefit both yourself and others.

- Third, develop a healthier value system that will free you to take just actions.

Epictetus used the following story as a pure example of justice. "What man among us does not admire the saying of Lycurgus the Lacedaemonian? For when he had been blinded in one eye by one of his fellow-citizens, and the people had turned over the young man to him, to take whatever vengeance upon the culprit he might desire, this he refrained from doing, but brought him up and made a good man of him, and presented him in the theatre. And when the Lacedaemonians expressed their surprise, he said, 'This man when I received him at your hands was insolent and violent; I am returning him to you a reasonable and public-spirited person.'"

This example is the height of Stoic justice, in which the wronged person works to heal the offender rather than demand punishment. That sense of justice may be far outside your reach. But what can you do now to take actions that benefit everyone?

Reserve Clause

How can you take an action and remain centered if it doesn't work out? You learn to use the Stoic reserve clause. "I will weed my garden this afternoon, if nothing prevents it." That ending phrase, "if nothing prevents it," is powerful. I can't say for certain that

I will get to weed my garden this afternoon: It could rain; a more pressing issue could come up. If I don't get to weed that garden, but I said I would, I might actually get frustrated when things don't work out. You can, of course, come up with many projects more important than gardening. "If nothing prevents it" allows space for the Stoic perspective. I want to do x, I understand that I don't control that outcome. If you use the reserve clause consistently, you'll find stability even when life shakes a project or two.

A love of humanity shapes all Stoic actions. The early Stoics considered each of us to be part of a single organism, as though we were all individual cells that make up a body. Marcus Aurelius said we were made to work together like the top and bottom row of teeth. He also said that acting against others was a seditious act, ripping us apart from our natural community. In the next chapter we will discuss Justice and expand on our love of people.

REFLECTION

"Do your best to convince them. But act on your own, if justice requires it. If met with force, then fall back on acceptance and peaceability. Use the setback to practice other virtues. Remember that our efforts are subject to circumstances, you weren't aiming to do the impossible. Aiming to do what then? To try. And you succeeded. What you set out to do is accomplished."

—MARCUS AURELIUS, *MEDITATIONS* 6:50

When does a Stoic stop? Why abandon a project when you see the world as indifferent and have the courage to act despite obstacles? In this quote, Marcus Aurelius points out that there are times when resistance to our actions will force a reevaluation of our options. He presents two practices as solutions to the dilemma, which we've named *infinite opportunity* and the *reserve clause*. Infinite opportunity reminds us that every challenge presents a chance to practice virtue. The emperor uses his failed attempt to enact justice as an opportunity to practice acceptance and peaceability. He also uses the reserve clause to show that he never actually failed. He hoped for a particular outcome, but he also wanted to act well and to remain his best self. His goal was to do his best and—at this—he succeeded.

When you have to decide whether to abandon a particular project or not, ask yourself two things:

- Have I done the best that I could?

- In this new situation, what opportunities do I have to be my best self? After this, do what wisdom tells you is best.

Two Missions

You've already learned the *reserve clause,* but that's not the only short phrase that can quickly align you with Stoic thinking. I call this next practice, *two missions.* The Stoic mind-set allows you to live life, challenges and all, while remaining happy. It is helpful to have a technique that reminds you of your goal to live a virtuous and satisfying life. Here's an example.

Think about driving. There may be traffic, you might get cut off, or make a wrong turn. Remind yourself that you want to drive, but you also want to remain content in life.

Whenever you get ready to do anything, think about what's coming and what obstacles could pop up. Then add a phrase about your higher goal: "I also want to be content" or "I want to be in harmony with life" or "I want to protect my best self."

Two Handles

> *"Everything has two handles: one by which it can be carried and another by which it cannot. If your brother acts unjustly, do not take hold of the situation by the handle of injustice, for by that it can't be carried; but rather by the opposite, knowing that he is your brother, that he is family, and you will carry it successfully."*

—Epictetus, *Enchiridion* 43

The metaphor of *two handles* will remind you that your approach to a challenge is a choice. In Epictetus's example, you can repay injustice with injustice, or you can choose to be your better self. This is always your choice. In any situation, particularly those that are challenging, remind yourself that there are two ways to engage, and pick the better one.

The Morning Orientation

We will get to loving other people, but for now, I would like you to work on just putting up with them. Marcus Aurelius has a powerful morning meditation that will help you practice Stoicism from the moment you wake up. Read the following quote by him, from *Meditations* 2:1, and adapt it to your own voice. Begin your morning with these thoughts and, when you feel overwhelmed, remind yourself of them again.

When you wake up in the morning, tell yourself: The people I deal with today will be meddling, ungrateful, arrogant, dishonest, jealous, and surly. They are like this because they can't tell good from evil. But I have seen the beauty of good, and the ugliness of evil, and have recognized that the wrongdoer has a nature related to my own—not of the same blood and birth, but the same mind, and possessing a share of the divine. And so none of them can hurt me. No one can implicate me in ugliness. Nor can I feel angry at my relative, or hate him. We were born to work together like feet, hands, and eyes, like the two rows of teeth, upper and lower. To obstruct each other is unnatural. To feel anger at someone, to turn your back on him: These are unnatural.

Think of someone you know, or just know of, who seems to choose their actions based on everyone's good, not just their own. What do you believe drives their decisions?

THE DISCIPLINE OF ASSENT: ACCEPTING YOURSELF

> *"People feel disturbed not by things, but by the views they take of them."*

—Epictetus, *Enchiridion* 5

The Discipline of Assent trains you to pay attention to your thought process and cultivate a healthy mind. Assent, in Stoicism, means saying yes to information you have received. Stoicism asks you to pause and think about your responses to life, rather than allowing instinct and habit to run your life.

There's a story of a Stoic teacher who was traveling by boat when a huge storm threatened to capsize the ship and drown the crew. A fellow passenger noticed that the Stoic got pale just like everyone else, but unlike the rest, he never showed fear. After the storm ended, the passenger questioned the

Stoic. "It looked like you were frightened, I saw your face get pale. Isn't that against your teaching?" The Stoic explained that our initial reactions aren't up to us, they are natural responses to a sudden event. What Stoicism had taught the teacher was to only accept the fact that a storm was happening. Other thoughts, such as "this is dangerous" or "we're going to drown," he never accepted, instead choosing to focus on keeping everyone afloat. Learning to guide your thought process in this way will allow you to put stresses aside and focus your energy on what you control.

The Discipline of Assent requires your attention. Stoics saw assent as a three-step process:

- **First, something happens to you (initial impression).**

- **Next, you recognize what happened (objective representation).**

- **Finally, you add your own spin on events (value judgment).**

It's a simple process, but without training, this process often leads us astray. You have already learned multiple techniques, from short phrases to longer meditations, that require you to understand when to use them. If you don't notice the tension you're holding in your body as someone says something harsh, how will you make it go away?

Take this example. While home alone, you hear a noise outside. Hearing that noise and feeling your gut reaction is the initial impression. The objective representation is when your brain says, "I just heard a noise outside." So far so good, you simply recognized the reality of the event without adding to it. What if your next step, the value judgment, leads you to say, "I'm in danger"? You added this thought and it is not necessarily true. It's here, during the value judgment, where you can begin to build anxiety and stress by thinking unhealthy thoughts. The Discipline of Assent asks you to pause at step 2. Take in the objective representation, but say no to any other thoughts that start to build on that impression. Instead, give yourself space to better judge the situation.

You Are Just an Appearance!

"You are just an appearance and not at all the thing you appear to be." This is a phrase given to us by Epictetus specifically to help with the Discipline of Assent. Whenever an overwhelming value judgment forms in your mind, pause and repeat that line. Say no to the judgment until you've examined it further.

Bracketing

Another method to the Discipline of Assent is to *bracket* the initial impression, meaning you separate it from everything else, for the purpose of suspending judgment. Look at the event clearly, take it at face value. After this, you can "say something more." Ask basic Stoic questions such as, "Is it under my control?" This allows for a clearer head and a more reasoned judgment.

Circle Yourself

The exercise is similar to *circle the present* from the Discipline of Desire. Now you are bringing to mind what is most important about yourself, your ability to control your thoughts, actions, desires, and aversions. Mentally separate this aspect of yourself from the rest of the world, reminding yourself that this part of you alone is fully under your control. Take a moment and think only about this part of yourself; your will that directs your thoughts and actions. Free yourself from outer influences so that you can choose the best action for you.

Wisdom is the virtue associated with the Discipline of Assent. In light of what you have just learned, how do you see wisdom relating to these practices?

IN THE MOMENT

Review the previous exercises. Which of these can you use throughout your day, and which work better as scheduled practices?

_____

_____

_____

_____

_____

_____

_____

_____

ASSENT, DESIRE, AND ACTION

In reality, life is messy, and the disciplines don't stay separate. Most challenges require you to make proper use of assent, focus your desires in the right way, and take the best action possible.

What if a stranger yells at you? You might startle or turn red. You'll have to draw on practices like *you are just an appearance* and *bracketing* to keep from making bad judgments. The Discipline of Desire reminds you not to avoid conflict, but to avoid *a bad reaction* to conflict. You can remind yourself that this is one of the *infinite opportunities* to practice virtue. As you choose those actions, the *two missions* will center you, and, if you practiced the *morning meditation*, you might even say, "Hey, I knew this might happen and I'm prepared."

The disciplines can be practiced separately, setting aside time to work on each, but in the day-to-day, you will need to choose the best practice for each situation. The more you practice, the more your tools will be ready at hand when you need them. That consistency will help you overcome challenges and remain in harmony as you move through the day.

"Here is what is enough for you: the judgment you are bringing to bear at this moment upon reality, as long as it is objective, the action you are carrying out at this moment, as long as it is accomplished in the service of the human community; and the inner disposition in which you find yourself at this moment, as long as it is a disposition of joy in the face of the conjunction of events caused by extraneous causality."

—Marcus Aurelius, *Meditations* 9:6

Take a moment to decide how you would like to practice the disciplines. What exercise would you like to practice tomorrow to begin incorporating the Stoic mind-set?

THE OPPOSITE OF DISCIPLINE

Philosophical techniques are helpful, but they aren't the end goal. Stoicism isn't a checklist. You can't simply mark off the practices you've tried once and say, "That's it, I've conquered Stoicism." Instead, probe your mind. Are your intentions virtuous? Are you gaining perspectives on your actions? Are you thriving? If so, you're exercising the disciplines effectively.

Note that, as you improve, you may be tempted to demand the same from other people. Refrain from that urge. Instead, keep the standard you develop for yourself personal. Unfortunately, I've seen self-proclaimed Stoics pick people apart for their lack of reason or their willingness to accept negative emotions. A person looking for help on a Stoic forum might admit, "I'm struggling with anxiety and I don't know what to do." Responses sometimes amount to "just stop being anxious" or even, "stop being so weak." I hope you can already see the insensitivity in these responses. Epictetus said, "Whatever, then, we shall discover to be at the same time affectionate and also consistent with reason, this we confidently declare to be right and good." As you grow in your reasoning, it's important to also stretch your compassion, rather than to shame others for not taking the same path.

You are about to leave behind the formality of discipline for the art of virtue. The exercises you've done have a goal, to lead you to personal excellence, also called virtue. Stoics consider virtue the only absolute good, the only thing that is always healthy, the only path that will constantly allow you to thrive. Bring your knowledge of the disciplines with you as we look at the true focus of those mental practices.

CHAPTER 4:
Acting Like a Stoic

> *"Never stop sculpting your own statue, until the splendor of virtue shines out."*

—Plotinus, *Enneads*

Stoic Actions

In the previous chapter, you learned tools to help you do the work of living. Now, you will uncover the kind of work you are meant to do. What do you look like at your best? How do you feel? What actions do you take? How do you relate to other people? As we uncover virtue, you'll begin to visualize what personal excellence looks like to you.

Virtue means excellence, the best example of who you can be. The Stoics had many metaphors to describe it. One of my favorites comes from Cicero, who said the Stoics referred to virtue as, "ripeness." Ripe fruit is fruit at its best, but fruit is only ripe for a moment. Ripeness is a striking metaphor for the Stoic view of virtue. Moral virtue, like ripeness, is also a thing that cannot be saved up—you can't bank some virtue on Monday to withdraw later in the week. You can only be virtuous, or excellent, in the moment. A minute later and you might find excellence again, or you could fail. You have endless opportunities to exercise virtue.

Modern philosopher Pierre Hadot defines the virtues as follows:

- **Wisdom, "the science of what ought or ought not to be done."**

- **Courage, "the science of what ought or ought not be tolerated."**

- **Justice, "the science of what ought and ought not be distributed."**

- **Moderation, "the science of what ought or ought not to be chosen."**

The ancient Stoic school referred to their teachings as science, but virtue isn't found in a formula: It is an art. The basics of virtue can be taught, but you have to do the work—both to improve, and to learn to express yourself through that work.

Stoic Virtues

The practices found within the disciplines exist to hone your virtue; their structure is important, but only if you use it to live up to your potential. A ballet dancer practices every day, but her art is found through the melding of technical skill and personal expression. Working on virtue will open you up to the art of living.

The Stoics inherited the four virtue categories—Wisdom, Courage, Justice, and Moderation—from a deeper history. Plato described the virtues in a similar way to the later Stoics, yet the Stoics insisted that virtues were not separate, like different species, but instead intertwined as a whole. The virtues implied one another: Wisdom is necessary for Justice. Justice informs Moderation, and so on. Still, thinking about the particular expressions of virtue will help you find clarity around your choices. So let's look at these virtues and find ways to bring them into your life.

WISDOM

Wisdom (*sophia*) is most closely associated with the Discipline of Assent. Stoics consider Wisdom a practical art, and, to reflect this, it's sometimes translated as *prudence*. Wisdom stands in opposition to thoughtlessness. You are wise when you take deliberate, reasoned actions that lead to a good flow in life. As you think about Wisdom, it might be helpful to see how it was further subdivided into the following:

- **good sense**

- **good calculation**

- **quick-wittedness**

- **discretion**

- **resourcefulness**

The primary role of Wisdom is to lead you to the good: to focus your attention on healthy thoughts, opinions, desires, and aversions. Wisdom's other role is to guide your decisions concerning the stuff of life. Should I choose this or that; do this or that?

Wisdom requires consistent mental attention. You must strive to examine your thought process. Practicing Wisdom requires understanding that you don't have to accept the first reaction that pops into your mind. Instead, you can build a space between your reaction and your next steps. Looking back at the Discipline of Assent, you can see how closely those practices and this virtue align.

Consider this: Who exemplifies practical Wisdom in your life, and what about this person stands out to you?

WISDOM EXERCISE: PHYSICAL DEFINITION

This exercise attempts to strip away your personal— and perhaps irrational—feelings concerning your desires. When you think about something you want, it helps to have a clear idea of it. Those expensive sneakers you want? They're only shoes: leather meant to protect your feet. If you buy them they will wear out, get stained, and eventually become trash. Are shoes really worth stressing over? Epictetus asked his students to imagine they had a favorite cup. What is it on the most basic level? It's ceramic. It holds drinks. It's breakable. He told them to leave behind thoughts of "it's painted so beautifully" and "it was a birthday present," so they could see it as just a cup. A cup that, if broken, isn't worth losing your good flow of life.

When anything presents itself to you, particularly if it seems in some way overwhelming, stop and define it at its most basic. Do not add value judgments. Clear away its mystique so that you can move forward with a clear head.

COURAGE

Courage (*andreia*) is mastery over your fears. It stands in opposition to cowardice. Courage is one of two virtues that are linked to the Discipline of Desire. If you no longer focus your desires and aversions toward the external world, but instead strive for virtue, you will unleash the power to act against the intolerable. The Stoics break Courage down into the following:

- endurance

- confidence

- high-mindedness

- cheerfulness

- industriousness

Think of some of the things you avoid. I used to avoid emotional conflict. Conflict brought me anxiety, so I learned to either pretend I was fine, or to do the bare minimum to get back to the status quo. This horrible strategy in both my personal and professional life led to negative results. Tensions festered until inevitably they blew up in my face. Stoicism taught me that other people's reactions weren't my direct responsibility. I could only control how I thought and acted, and if I did that well, the likelihood of others acting better also increased. The Stoic mind-set gave me Courage. I no longer avoided the reactions of others. Instead, I avoided cowardice, hesitation, and dread. I did that by striving both to be my best in every situation and to make the best out of every situation. As you practice the Discipline of Desire and Aversion, you will gain Courage. Remember, nothing can be bad for you if you do what is right according to your nature and do your best to accept your circumstances.

Consider this: Remember a time in your life when you displayed Courage. What about that moment brought Courage out?

COURAGE EXERCISE: PREMEDITATION OF CHALLENGES

Seneca once wrote, "Something already anticipated comes as less of a shock." A common Stoic practice involves visualizing the worst possible scenario. This helps clear your head. When you view the challenge from a Stoic point of view, if a similar event occurs in the future, you can more easily concentrate on living virtuously.

Envision an event you'd like to avoid. What specific details make this event a concern? Are they under your control? If not, what is in your control? How could you best meet this challenge? Who would you be after you survived it?

JUSTICE

Justice (*diakaiosunê*) relates to the Discipline of Action. Stoic Justice is broader than our common definition of the word; it means more than just abiding by the law. Stoics sometimes translate it as *morality*, as it encompasses all of your interactions with others. Stoicism teaches that all people are valuable and that we are meant to work together. Stoic Justice helps you to work with others, even if they are opposed to it.

Chrysippus (quoted by Cicero in *De Officiis*) provides part of the picture in this quote, "He who is running a race ought to endeavor and strive to the utmost of his ability to come off victor; but it is utterly wrong for him to trip up his competitor, or to push him aside. So in life it is not unfair for one to seek for himself what may accrue to his benefit; but it is not right to take it from another." In this example, we are in competition with others, but we make sure that the competition is fair.

Justice equates to cooperation. As Marcus Aurelius says, "We are made for cooperation, like feet, like hands, like eyelids, like the rows of the upper and lower teeth. To act against one another then is contrary to nature." We find this connection in some of the words the Stoics chose to describe Justice:

- **honesty**
- **equity**
- **fair-dealing**
- **goodwill**
- **benevolence**
- **kindness**

Exhibiting fairness toward friends comes naturally, but what about enemies? Stoicism says we shouldn't be angry or hateful toward those who wrong us. It is a Stoic maxim that no one is voluntarily evil. If a person insults you or steals from you, they did it because they thought they were doing something good for themselves. Epictetus says a Stoic will be "patient, gentle, delicate, and forgiving, as he would toward someone in a state of ignorance, who missed the mark when it came to the most important things. He will not be harsh to anyone, for he will have perfectly understood Plato's words: 'Every soul is deprived of the truth against its will.'"

Consider this: How would your relationships change if your actions came from the Stoic understanding of Justice?

JUSTICE EXERCISE: THE ARCHER

When we work for Justice, we often want a particular outcome. In Stoicism, your actions must be just, even if you never achieve the outcomes you're hoping for. An image that can help develop this mind-set is The Archer. Picture an archer. She chooses a target. She draws her bow. She releases the arrow. What part of this situation does the archer control? A gust of wind could move the arrow off target. The target could move. The archer must focus, not on striking the target, but on shooting straight.

This is a picture of virtue. As you aim for just outcomes, realize that what you control are your intentions and the actions that come from them. Focusing on your own actions will give you the best chance of reaching external goals.

MODERATION

Moderation (*sôphrosunê*) is control over desires and, along with Courage, it is an expected outcome of practicing the Discipline of Desire. Moderation stands in opposition to excess. If you desire only virtue, then you can be reasonable in what you want and generous with what you have been given. Moderation can be divided into:

- **appropriateness**

- **modesty**

- **self-control**

The Stoics viewed life as a banquet. Picture yourself at a party where the host went all out with the food and drink. Imagine expensive wines, mouthwatering dishes, and decadent desserts. Everyone's grabbing plates and glasses and heading over to get their fill. How are you going to act? Are you going to pile your plate high so you don't miss out on anything? Will you fill up your glass knowing there's not enough of that particular wine for everyone to try? If you miss out on the dessert you had your eye on, will it ruin your night? If you get to it in time, will you take so much that others don't get to enjoy it? Epictetus says that a Stoic won't desire that dessert before they have it and therefore won't be disturbed if they never get it. If the dessert does arrive, they won't take so much that others will be left without. Also, if they really grasp Stoicism, they might choose to let the dessert pass even though it arrives. That Stoic, Epictetus claims, is worthy of ruling with the gods! The banquet metaphor is meant to apply to all of your interactions. If you direct your desire toward being your best self, you won't focus on getting things, but on using the things you already have.

Another way to understand moderation is to think of yourself as a guest in someone else's house. How do you treat things when you know you're only borrowing them? All things are impermanent. What you have today will be used up, might break or be taken away, and won't be yours forever. If you live as if things are permanent, in a world where that is never true, it will hurt to lose them. That hurt comes from unrealistic thoughts. If you assume that good health is your right, then even a simple cold will seem unjust and cause you to act poorly. If you believe your job will last forever, a layoff will devastate you. It doesn't have to be this way. If you accept that things are only yours for a time, then you can be happy you had them while you did and not fall apart when they're gone.

Consider this: Can you identify an area in your life where Moderation would have a large impact?

MODERATION EXERCISE: AMOR FATI

As you recall from the Discipline of Desire, the love of fate is a key mind-set for building Moderation into your life.

Take a moment to recall a time when things did not go the way you wanted but did end up working out in the end. In what ways did the challenge disrupt your positive emotions? In hindsight, can you apply a Stoic mind-set to the situation? How does that mind-set affect your desires and your aversions?

THE OPPOSITE OF VIRTUE

As you discover what virtue means to you, it's helpful to have something to measure yourself against. In one of his letters, Seneca describes Stoicism like this, "No school has more goodness and gentleness; none has more love for human beings, nor more attention to the common good. The goal which it assigns to us is to be useful, to help others, and to take care, not only of ourselves, but of everyone in general and of each one in particular." It can be difficult to spot your own flaws. You don't have the benefit of a Stoic teacher who can point out your weak areas and push you to do better. From time to time, return to Seneca's description. Are you becoming someone who fits this description? If you are, you're doing a great job. Keep it up.

IN THE MOMENT

The Stoics would look for models of virtue in the people they knew, in famous figures of the past, and even from myth.

What person, or even fictional character, best exemplifies a well-lived life to you?

INDIFFERENTS

When Stoics say, "virtue is the only good," they mean it. Stoics place everything else, everything that isn't a moral opinion, thought, or action, into a category called the "indifferents." This isn't an emotional category, to be confused with "indifference"; you are never asked to disengage from life. Categorizing everything outside of our control as an indifferent says you recognize that such things, in themselves, can't provide lasting happiness. Still, you live life and have to make decisions about how to live your life. Stoicism says that there are things that, all being equal, it would make sense to prefer over others. Health and physical well-being over illness, for instance. They call those things that usually benefit us *preferred indifferents* and things that are often detrimental to people *dispreferred indifferents*.

Here's a list of indifferent things given by Epictetus:

- **your body**

- **your property**

- **your reputation**

- **your job**

- **everything else that isn't your own doing**

But don't these things matter? Of course they do! But their value is significantly different than virtue's value. Wisdom is always to your benefit. Courage will always help you. Your job? It's helpful to receive a paycheck, but a job can also make demands on your time that can harm your well-being. You'd think your own body would be pretty directly involved in your happiness—and it is! But you might also recall moments in which your body, or how you chose to use it, was a detriment to your life. Stoic indifferents give you clarity. Recognizing something as an indifferent helps you look past the thing itself and toward how you use it. Your choices about indifferent things contribute to a healthy life.

I have asked you many times to divide things into what is in your control and what is not in your control. That exercise separates *you* from indifferents. As you grow in that practice, you will understand the things you do not control also don't have to control you: Your opinions, thoughts, and actions are yours to choose, and no one and nothing can influence them without your consent. This will change your relationship to indifferents; you'll find that their value isn't found within them but is based in how you choose to use them.

REFLECTION

"If you do not know to which port you are sailing, then no wind is favorable."

—SENECA, *LETTERS FROM A STOIC* 71

You are trying to bring out your best self. In different areas of life—your thoughts (Assent), your wants (Desire), and your choices (Action)—you try for excellence at all times. It may help to visualize this outstanding you, your virtuous self.

- Whom do you see when you imagine your best self?

- What is standing between you and this "other" you?

- What steps can you take to come closer to this vision? A final reminder: Stoicism says that your virtuous self already exists, you can choose that version of you right now if you choose.

WHAT ARE YOUR PRINCIPLES?

The disciplines and virtues have given you an understanding of the Stoic mind-set, with its particular principles and priorities. What are yours? What do you value most? What are you striving for? As you think about this, are the actions you have been taking the right actions to get you where you want to go?

What parts of Stoic thinking most closely match what you already believe? What led you to these beliefs?

What parts of Stoic thinking challenge your present principles? What would you have to change to practice a more Stoic mind-set?

_____

_____

_____

_____

_____

_____

_____

_____

_____

_____

_____

_____

Virtues Evaluation

Take a moment to consider your daily interactions. On a scale of 1–5, with 1 meaning, "not at all," and 5 meaning, "consistently," how well do you display each of the virtues in your life?

Wisdom _____

Courage _____

Justice _____

Moderation _____

In part 3, you will use what you have learned to cultivate positivity, disrupt negativity, and uncover your best self as we look more deeply at Stoic psychology. You'll discover more methods to shape your emotional life. You'll also get more personal and look at your relationships with family, friends, and the rest of the world. All of this requires you to bring the disciplines and virtues with you, so you can take these methods off the page and turn them into something impactful. Let's dive in.

PART III

STOICISM FOR LIFE

CHAPTER 5:
Cultivating Positivity

> *"True happiness is to enjoy the present, without anxious dependence upon the future, not to amuse ourselves with either hopes or fears but to rest satisfied with what we have, which is sufficient, for he that is so wants nothing. The greatest blessings of human-kind are within us and within our reach. A wise person is content with their lot, what-ever it may be, without wishing for what they have not."*

—Seneca, *On the Happy Life*

Positive Thoughts

Both the Greeks and the Romans believed in and worshipped the goddess Fortune, a beautiful, blind woman who would hand out and take away gifts from the people she met. In a story called "The Tablet of Cebes," Fortune is seen among a crowd of both sad and joyful people. The happy ones had just received her gifts and called her "Good Fortune." The ones who lost their gifts were despondent and named her "Bad Fortune." The Stoics would say that if you build your emotional life around Fortune's gifts, then there will be nothing constant in your life. How can you have any assurance of happiness if it can be snatched away at any moment? Wouldn't it be better to find a secure happiness? Stoicism trains you to move your emotional well-being away from Fortune's indifferent gifts and to re-center it on virtue, your own best efforts in life, which is firmly within your own control.

In this chapter, you will learn how drawing on the disciplines and focusing on your virtue will cultivate positivity. You will develop a mental practice that allows for contentment, joy, and love to flourish. You'll do this by gaining an even deeper understanding of what you can control, so you can tackle life's responsibilities without letting them shake your emotions.

Focus: What You Can Control

> *"Some things are in our control and others not. Things in our control are opinion, pursuit, desire, aversion, and, in a word, whatever are*

our own actions. Things not in our control are body, property, reputation, our social position, and, in one word, whatever are not our own actions."

—Epictetus, *Enchiridion* 1

We've talked constantly about "what we control," but let's home in on this idea. The quote contains the first lines of the *Enchiridion*, a handbook developed from Epictetus's teachings. This practice, separating what we control from what we do not, is foundational to the Stoic outlook. We call it the Dichotomy of Control. Every Stoic practice requires you to separate what you control from everything else, and everything else is a lot!

Epictetus gives us four categories that you control directly:

- **your opinions about life**

- **what you pursue in life**

- **what you want**

- **what you do not want**

These are all linked to another term I've used before: value judgments. Your values, and what you try to do because of those values, remain intimately yours.

Everything else lies outside of your control, in the category of indifferents. Epictetus begins his list of indifferents with your own body. Your body is, of course, quite closely related to what you control, but can you always guarantee its health? Could a disease or injury take away some control? When Stoics talk about control, they mean *fully* under your control. Therefore, even your own body is an indifferent because circumstances could change your ability to use it. The final half of chapter 1 of the *Enchiridion*, written by Epictetus, explains the rationale:

> *"The things in our control are by nature free, unrestrained, unhindered; but those not in our control are weak, slavish, restrained, belonging to others. Remember, then, that if you believe that things which are slavish by nature are also free, and that what belongs to others is your own, then you will be hindered. You will lament, you will be disturbed, and you will find fault both with gods and men. But if you suppose that only to be your own which is your own, and what belongs to others such as it really is, then no one will ever compel you or restrain you. Further, you will find fault with no one or accuse no one. You will do nothing against your will. No one will hurt you, you will have no enemies, and you will not be harmed."*

A middle ground of "sort of in your control" does not exist in the black-and-white practice of the Dichotomy of Control. Something is either 100 percent in your control or an indifferent. If you place your emotional well-being in something that Fortune can take from you, or will never give you, you'll always remain vulnerable to the ups and downs of life. If, instead, you derive happiness from things that you possess, you can enjoy happiness and the gifts life does give you while you have them.

Everything you've learned so far will help you focus on what you control:

- **The Discipline of Desire transfers your affections from *things* in life to your virtue, how you walk through life.**

- **The Discipline of Action tells you to stop seeking a particular end goal and instead make your best move at every step.**

- **The Discipline of Assent helps you overcome misinterpretations of your circumstances so you approach life with clarity.**

As you practice the disciplines, your mind will start to create room for positive emotions to flourish. Let's review a few more techniques to focus you on what you control.

IN THE MOMENT

*"Learn to ask of all actions, 'Why are they doing that?'
Starting with your own."*

—MARCUS AURELIUS, *MEDITATIONS* 10:37

Remember: The one thing you control is yourself. As you learn to seek out a good flow of life, look at your own choices first, before judging the actions of others.

Up to You

The Dichotomy of Control asks you to decide what is *really* up to you. In every situation, remind yourself that you own your value judgments and decisions—you control them. Your opinions, choices, desires, and aversions rest with you; everything else falls into the category of indifferent. By accepting this, you become free to act with excellence and virtue at all times. You will still use the indifferent things in life in the best way possible, but gaining or losing them won't affect your harmony. Remaining focused on the right things allows space for positivity and resilience in the face of life's ups and downs.

This Is Nothing to Me

Another phrase that Stoics keep at the ready is "This is nothing to me." Whenever anything begins to take up too much mental space, think of this phrase. For example, maybe tomorrow you're going to find out if you get a promotion. If the anticipation creates feelings of worry or anxiety, then it's stealing the positive emotions you could be experiencing right now. Therefore, reframe it: "This promotion is nothing to me." Meaning, the promotion will not affect your ability to live with virtue and to be the best you possible. The dramatic nature of "this is nothing to me" can bring your thoughts back to the Dichotomy of Control, to *circling* both yourself and the present, to disciplining desire and action and assent. You can't control that future thing, so don't let it impact your present happiness.

It Was Returned

> *"The only possession the wise person has is virtue, and of this they can never be robbed. Of all else they have merely the use on loan."*

—Seneca, *On the Firmness of the Wise Man*

Another phrase that will help you is, "It was returned." The Stoics taught that all indifferents should be viewed as on loan to you. Everything changes, everything is mortal, nothing goes on forever. How do these thoughts protect your positivity? Well, what gets you into trouble is acting as if things are permanent. If you expect a favorite thing to be yours forever, and it breaks, gets lost, or is stolen, that's when the negativity comes. Stoicism counsels you to say, "It was returned," whenever anything leaves or is lost, gone forever. This outlook, one of impermanence, protects you against the shock of change, and will also help you take full advantage of life's gifts when they are here. Accepting that nothing lasts forever will help you engage with things in the moment.

What Can You Control?

Thinking from a Stoic perspective, look at the following list and decide if it is in your control or outside of your control.

- **You are in a traffic jam.**

- **You are angry because you are late for work.**

- **Your friend is sad about a recent breakup.**

- **You are anxious about a presentation you have to give.**

- **Your child is sick.**

- **A tragedy has occurred in your community.**

- **You feel guilty about an action you took yesterday.**

- **Your flight is delayed.**

- **You are outraged by something you just read.**

- **Your arm is broken.**

TAKE RESPONSIBILITY

Knowing what you control doesn't free you from the obligations of life. You have to eat. You would prefer a roof over your head. You have friends and family that you love and whom you want to help. So, how can you interact with indifferents while not becoming overwhelmed by them? You already have many tools to draw upon! You've already learned the *reserve clause* and *two missions*, both of which help you move forward while remembering to remain your best self. *The archer* reminds you how to focus on your actions without obsessing over the outcome. *Premeditation of challenges* and *infinite opportunity* help you remain confident that no matter the challenges ahead, you can act with excellence. Stoicism allows you to take action without feeling weighed down by false expectations. The Dichotomy of Control is freeing this way: It reminds you that you cannot control outcomes but can only do your best. If you concentrate on your own actions, you know that you are doing everything you can to get what you want and find joy in that fact no matter the eventual result.

I worked as a shelter manager in New York City during Hurricane Sandy. At one shelter, donations included food that not all the clients could eat. Ham was mixed into everything, from the morning eggs to the evening's green beans, and a number of our families had religious objections to that ingredient. I requested that the food either be appropriate for everyone or varied to meet different needs. This didn't happen, so I refused to take the donations.

To me, this came down to a matter of justice. Every family in the shelter had lost their home and needed to save money. Providing meals allowed people to save, but part of the population had to purchase every meal, using up their resources. My job entailed serving everyone, and I could only do that if something changed. However, when I refused to take donations, my role as manager was threatened. I had to decide if taking the action I believed in outweighed keeping my job. I reminded myself that I only controlled whether or not I performed my job well—virtuously, as I saw it—and someone else held the responsibility to keep me on or let me go. So I stuck with my convictions.

Choosing the right action was deeply satisfying, and I rested in the knowledge that I had done my absolute best. In the end the meals were changed to meet everyone's needs, and I continued to serve as a manager. Both outcomes were what I'd wanted, but they remained outside my control—my own actions would have remained untarnished regardless of the end result.

Focusing your energy on what you can control while practicing the Stoic disciplines helps you find mental and emotional stability despite life's ups and downs. This frees you to engage with the world around you, secure in the knowledge that you can always thrive as long as you remain true to your virtue. Another benefit of a healthy mental outlook is that such a mind allows room for positive mental states to flourish. Let's look at that dynamic now.

IN THE MOMENT

There are times when things "go wrong," but you still find happiness because you stood strong, persevered, and stayed true to yourself.

- **Can you think of a time you did not get what you wanted, but you still found happiness because of who you were in the moment?**

- **What was it about your attitude or actions that gave you satisfaction?**

Cultivating Positive Thoughts

If you want to experience a flower's beauty for a day, you might pick one and place it in a vase. If you'd like access to that beauty all season long, it would be better to plant a garden. People often chase experiences, micromanage both their environment and the people around them, all in the hope that they'll get a spark of joy out of it all. This is like picking a flower: You might get something you want, but you can't keep it. If you want lasting happiness, instead, properly arrange what's inside you—not the things surrounding you. Not only can you experience joy, tranquility, goodwill, and so many other positive emotions: you can experience these states all the time.

The secret involves not aiming directly for happiness—because it isn't a destination. Happiness merely accompanies you on your journey when your travels are virtuous. You cultivate positivity by living the *good flowing life* that we discussed earlier. By working on yourself, you create a life in which good thoughts and feelings can thrive. Marcus Aurelius reminded himself of this whenever he felt out of step with the world. In *Meditations* 4:3 he wrote, "People try to get away from it all—to the country, to the beach, to the mountains. You always wish that you could too. Which is idiotic: You can get away from it anytime you like. By going within. Nowhere you can go is more peaceful—more free of interruptions—than your own soul. Especially if you have other things to rely on. An instant's recollection and there it is: complete tranquility. And by tranquility I mean a kind of harmony." Marcus Arelius says that peace will come easier if you have "other things to rely on." What constitutes those things? They are the very Stoic tools we've already discussed. Your first step toward cultivating positivity is to remind yourself to remain on the Stoic path.

> *"For every challenge, remember the resources you have within you to cope with it."*
>
> —Epictetus, *Enchiridion* 10

Whenever you are presented with an obstacle, start with self-assessment. Do you foresee a challenge? Then you have endurance. Is someone annoying? You have patience. Take a moment to draw on your own abilities, remembering to apply those energies only on what you can control. This attentiveness keeps you on the virtuous path where happiness resides. As you follow this course in life, you will enjoy the work of being yourself. Stoics place pride in moments when we're doing our best, because we can *always* choose to do our best. This puts your successes firmly under your control. If you can do this, then you can never really feel frustrated. The tranquility that comes from this mind-set creates the space where positivity flourishes.

Consistent Stoic practice develops your state of mind into one that allows positivity to grow. Thinking back on the Discipline of Assent, the Stoics say that first, something happens to you (initial impression). Next, you recognize what happened (objective representation). Finally, you add your own spin on events (value judgment). If you have unhealthy value judgments, you will experience the negative mental states (Stoics call these *passions*; more on this in chapter 6, page 105). If your values align with wisdom, you will experience *good passions*. The Stoics wrote about three good passions that flow from a rational mind that holds healthy value judgments. They called them Joy, Wish, and Caution.

JOY

Joy is a reasonable mental elation based on your proper judgments concerning life. Joy is delight, good cheer, and serenity. Joy is present-focused. You take Joy in the life you're presently living. If you confine your desires and aversions to the things you control, if you circle the present to be in the moment, then Joy bubbles up. If a friend visits, you enjoy the time you have with him. Yes, he will leave eventually, but you won't experience sadness, because you're in the moment and that moment is joyful. When your friend leaves, you feel grateful for the time you spent together, and seek new things to appreciate.

WISH

Wish, sometimes called "willing," means a reasonable striving for things in life. Striving is future-focused, and Wish involves our hopes for the future. This state of mind links to the Discipline of Action, in that your striving is socially directed; remember, the Stoic works for the good of the community, not just themselves. The Stoics subdivided Wish into affection, kindheartedness, and benevolence; words that illuminate the social aspect of this good passion as each of them relies upon your relationship to others. This emotional state is cultivated through practices like the reserve clause "if nothing prevents it." You have reasonable desires for the world and your future, but you're invested in *how* you work toward those goals, not specifically in the outcome.

CAUTION

Caution, also translated as discretion, is a reasonable avoidance of something in life. As you understand from earlier lessons, a Stoic is only meant to avoid vice, virtue's opposite. Another future-focused mental state, Caution helps you make reasonable plans for the future, knowing you can take part in anything as long as you promote your virtue and avoid the possibility of vice. Imagine a large protest, one that you felt compelled to attend, but was rumored to become dangerous. Fear might prevent you from attending. Caution would say yes, it's preferable to be safe, but it's even better to promote justice. Your final choice would come down to which actions allow you to be your best self.

These positive mental states are bigger than emotion: If you consistently invoke Joy, Wish, and Caution, then positivity will grow out of them. At the same time, the consistency of the Stoic mind makes it much more difficult for negative emotions to thrive. If you focus your mind on virtue and remain properly disciplined, negative thoughts and feelings can't easily take root, and your daily practice will help you weed out anything that sneaks through.

> *"People feel disturbed not by things, but by the views they take of them."*
>
> —Epictetus, *Enchiridion* 5

> *"Today I escaped from anxiety. Or no, I discarded it, because it was within me, in my own perceptions—not outside."*
>
> —Marcus Aurelius, *Meditations* 9:13

"What is the happy life? It is peace of mind, and lasting tranquillity. This will be yours if you possess greatness of soul; it will be yours if you possess the steadfastness that resolutely clings to a good judgment just reached."

—Seneca, *On the Happy Life*

REFLECTION

"Let us go to our sleep with joy and gladness; let us say 'I have lived; the course which Fortune set for me is finished.' And if God is pleased to add another day, we should welcome it with glad hearts. A person is happiest, and is secure in his own possession of himself, who can await the morrow without apprehension. When a man has said: 'I have lived!', every morning he arises he receives a bonus."

−SENECA, *LETTERS FROM A STOIC* 12

The Stoics would often take their present-focused philosophy to the extreme and visualize each day as their final day. Seneca claims that this practice can free you of anxiety about the future, allowing you to wake up and receive the new day as a gift. This evening, test Seneca's technique and treat today as an ending, a clean break from the future.

When you are ready to sleep, say to yourself, "I have lived; the course which Fortune set for me is finished." Use this thought to break any threads of anxiety that lead off into tomorrow.

Thinking ahead to tomorrow, what would it mean for the day to be truly fresh? What if the day was not a continuation of past projects and challenges, but a pure, new thing? Who could you be during that new day?

As you cultivate positivity, you also build emotional resilience. If you focus on virtue, you will be naturally resistant to unhealthy thoughts, because anger, fear, despair, and the like all come from incorrect value judgments. In the next chapter, we will look more closely at the darker side of life, so you can use your tools to combat negative thinking when it happens and, ideally, learn to stop such thoughts and feelings before they happen.

CHAPTER 6:
Practicing Emotional Resilience

"The invulnerable thing is not something that is never struck, but something that is never hurt; by this mark I will show you the wise person."

—Seneca, *On the Firmness of the Wise Man*

Taming Negative Thoughts

In this chapter, you will focus your tools—the disciplines and virtues—on something everyone struggles with: negative thinking. You will learn to tame negative thoughts and even totally discard them, and you'll discover that emotional resilience and cultivating positive emotions are two sides of one coin. Everyone faces challenges, but we each get to decide how to respond to them. By focusing your energy on that which you can control and valuing your virtue over everything else, you can stay positive in the toughest circumstances. And when negativity slips in? You bounce back and quickly get back to the good flow of life.

When Bad Things Happen

Stoic emotional theory always goes back to value judgments. You've already learned how hoping for indifferents can be harmful. In the same way, negative emotions emerge when you focus your desires or aversions on the wrong things. For example, you get angry when you can't have what you want; you feel sad when you lose things. The only way to break this cycle is to redirect your attention onto what you already own and what can never be taken from you: your virtue. If you approach life in this manner, you not only harness emotional resilience in an ever-changing world, but you will continue to cultivate positivity. With this in mind, let's tackle negativity with every tool Stoicism provides.

IN THE MOMENT

Certain situations or even particular people may always seem to bring out the worst in you.

- At this point in time, what circumstance has the tendency to push you toward negative thinking?

- Which Stoic tools can you apply in this situation to overcome these unhealthy attitudes?

Cultivating Emotional Resilience

"Some things strike the wise person, such as bodily pain and weakness, the loss of friends and children, and the ruin of his country in war-time, but they will not shake his principles. I do not say that the wise person does not feel these strikes, for we do not ascribe to him the hardness of stone or iron; there is no virtue if one is not conscious of what was endured. What then does he? He receives some blows, but when he has received them he rises above them, heals them, and brings them to an end; the more trivial things he does not even feel, nor does he make use of his accustomed

fortitude in the endurance of evil against them, but either takes no notice of them or considers them to deserve to be laughed at."

—Seneca, *On the Firmness of the Wise Man*

If you were perfectly wise, in the Stoic way, you would never experience negative states of mind, because your thoughts would always be healthy. This person, whom the Stoics call "the Sage," feels her initial impressions like anyone else, but makes healthy value judgments and therefore never succumbs to feelings of anger, despondence, fear, or the like. The Sage is an ideal, and we—of course—are not perfect. We will continue to make mistakes, but, practicing Stoicism, we can make real progress over time.

The same tools that cultivate positivity also help banish negativity. Fear tells you to avoid a hard conversation with a friend; the Dichotomy of Control and the Discipline of Action tell you that these conversations are indifferents and that you have to try to help the people in your life. Jealousy tells you to want what someone else has, but the Discipline of Desire reminds you that you have everything you need to be content. The key is constant practice. You have to continually use your tools so that, ideally, negativity never takes root. If it does, you are aware enough to recognize and deal with it.

In a letter titled "On Anger," Seneca says that, "The best plan is to reject straightway the first incentives to anger, to resist its very beginnings, and to take care not to be betrayed into it: for if once it begins to carry us away, it is hard to get back again into a healthy condition." He goes on to point out that you don't get to adjust your thinking from the outside, since you are your mind. If you are angry, that anger is part of your mind-set; it's hard to stop because the anger is now part of the very process that would stop it. Your best hope is to stand strong in Stoic philosophy. Remember that indifferents are "nothing to you" and no one took something from you—"it was returned." This challenge is a new opportunity to practice virtue. If you rest in these techniques, you will keep negativity at bay.

When negativity slips past your Stoic defenses, first recognize that you are stepping out of harmony with life. The Discipline of Assent will help you pay attention to your thoughts and weed out anything that no longer serves you. If an event brings up negative feelings, you can say, "you are just an appearance" and return your mind to a more peaceful state. You can use Physical Definition to take away the mystique of whatever is overwhelming your desires or aversions and get back on a healthy path. You can *bracket* the challenge to give yourself the space to think more clearly. As you continue to practice, you move closer to Seneca's wise person: resilient to things that used to bother you. After enough practice, you won't even notice things that used to annoy you!

I used to be a get-the-last-word-in sort of person. It really bothered me if I didn't "win" a discussion. Over the years, Stoicism taught me to value how I conduct myself during conversations more than how the interaction ends. Did I say what I meant to say? Did I give people a chance to understand my point of view? Did I listen to everyone else with my honest attention? If so, I did my best. Nowadays, if someone tries to belittle me, misrepresent my point of view, or demand attention I don't owe them, I barely notice. I'm content, and everything else is someone else's issue. It's freeing!

Picture someone cutting in front of you in a line. How would you feel? Maybe first you'd feel angry. After all, this person should know better. Before you run with this feeling, take into account your *two missions*—you need to stand in this line, and you also need to maintain harmony. Will you let this person take away your happiness? Of course not. He cannot take your happiness; only you can, when you indulge in a mistaken value judgment. So, you choose to remain content. But you can still address the person's mistake (as long as you feel safe doing so). He shouldn't have cut in front of you. The important thing is that, if you choose to confront the person, you do so with virtue, at your best, and not under the influence of what the Stoics call *passions*. And speaking of passions, let's look more closely at the Stoic view of negative states of mind.

REFLECTION

"Cling tooth and nail to the following rule: Not to give in to adversity, never to trust prosperity, and always to take full note of Fortune's habit of behaving just as she pleases, treating her as if she were actually going to do everything it is in her power to do. Whatever you have been expecting for some time comes as less of a shock."

—SENECA, *LETTERS FROM A STOIC* 78

Change is inevitable. The Stoics tell us that everything must change or nothing new could come out of life. They consider people foolish whenever they're shocked by change. How could you not know change was coming? It's everywhere, after all. In Seneca's line he tells you not to yield in the face of challenges and also not to expect simpler times to last forever. You are meant to remain in harmony no matter the ups and downs of life.

- What tools do you have to thrive during times of adversity?

- **What tools do you have that allow you to happily accept the good things of life, while recognizing those things will inevitably change?**

Negative Emotions

The Stoics refer to negative states of mind as *passions*. They consider passions to be diseases of the mind that need to be cured. You have already been introduced to the *good passions*, so I hope it's clear you're not being asked to be passionless, or cold to life. Passions, in Stoic language, are mental states based on mistaken value judgments. Passions are out of harmony with life. They cannot lead to thriving, because they take you in the wrong direction. For instance, you feel fear because you want to avoid something, but Stoicism tells you that that "something" is an indifferent and not worth fearing. You feel distress because you can't get something that, likewise, isn't worth worrying about. Passions are always mistakes. Stoicism trains you to avoid making the mistake altogether, if you can, and to correct yourself once you notice you're on the wrong path. The Stoics list four main passions:

- Fear

- Appetite

- Pleasure

- Distress

Let's investigate them now.

Fear

Fear is the expectation of a coming evil, a shrinking of the mind. Some of the feelings that flow from fear are terror, hesitation, shame, shock, panic, and anguish. Fear is future-focused but focused on the wrong things. Shame, for instance, is a fear of disgrace, but who can disgrace you? If you act with virtue, no one can disgrace you, and no one can cause you to act without virtue. The opposite of Fear is the good passion, Caution, and the antidote to Fear is the consistent practice of the Discipline of Desire. The Dichotomy of Control also helps to overcome Fear. All Fears are built around indifferents. If you learn to see indifferent things as outside of your control, you will be released from fearing such things.

Appetite

Appetite is an irrational desire for an expected good. It's future-focused. Want, hatred, contention, anger, lust, wrath, and rage all fall under this passion. Appetite is about dissatisfaction with the world and an attempt to fix that feeling with indifferent things. You overcome Appetite, the twin of Fear, with the application of the Discipline of Desire. The good passion, Wish, lies opposite to Appetite. You can see how the Dichotomy of Control is also at the core of this problem. If you can learn to only desire your own virtuous actions in life, then you won't have an overwhelming appetite for indifferent things.

Pleasure

Pleasure is a mistaken elation over something that seems to be good in the here and now. It includes rejoicing at another's misfortune, self-gratification, and extravagant joy, which the Stoics referred to as a dissolution of virtue. Pleasure ties your well-being into the things you own or the particular moment at hand, all of which can be taken from you. Pleasure's opposite is Joy, the state of mind that finds positivity despite the impermanence of things.

It may seem odd that you can have a present-focused passion, since Stoicism often advises you to be in the moment. While Stoicism *does* ask you to focus on the here and now, you must do so in the right way. For example, my five-year-old often cries whenever her friends have to go home. I give her a 10-minute warning or use other parenting techniques, but when the moment comes for them to part, she's devastated. She's invested her happiness in the present state of things, but those things (including the moment) are indifferents. The present-focused Stoic would instead concentrate on the things she controls. She would not seek pleasure in indifferents but would instead find joy in virtue. In fact, Pleasure's opposite is Joy, the state of mind that finds positivity despite the impermanence of things.

Concerning the wise person, Marcus Aurelius says in *Meditations* 10:11: "As to what any man shall say or think about him, or do against him, he never even thinks of it, being himself contented with these two things: with acting justly in what he now does, and being satisfied with what is now assigned to him." The passion of Pleasure can be uprooted by concentrating on excellence in every action, and in Amor Fati, the love and acceptance of your present moment.

Distress

The twin of Pleasure, Distress is an irrational contraction of the mind away from something already present. Malice, envy, jealousy, pity, grief, worry, sorrow, annoyance, vexation, and anguish all stem from Distress. Distress has no opposite passion. To overcome Distress is to allow space for all the other good passions to thrive. A technique I find particularly successful against Distress is one that I call "Festival."

FESTIVAL!

"When you're alone you should call this condition tranquility and freedom, and think of yourself like the gods; and when you are with many, you shouldn't call it a crowd, or trouble, or uneasiness, but festival and company, and contentedly accept it."

—EPICTETUS, *DISCOURSES* 1:12

I've been at loud concerts and had the time of my life. I've been at cafés where one conversation is slightly too loud and had my day ruined. Epictetus points out that we give a lot more grace to people at festivals than we do to folks on a regular day. He suggests we drop the idea of the crowd, and instead make every day a festival! Whenever the people around you begin to frustrate you—stop. Take a breath. Say, "festival." Think to yourself that, "This is a festival, these people are *my* people, I contentedly accept it."

Physical Definition and the Irrational

The Wisdom exercise you've already practiced, Physical Definition, is powerful against Pleasure and Appetite. Marcus Aurelius wrote about using this technique to demystify sex when he felt in danger of making decisions out of lust. He said that it is simply friction, a momentary spasm, and a sticky liquid—not the most flattering portrayal. If you want to build up the stable, good passion called Joy, you can't rest your happiness on things that can be taken from you or on future things that may never be. As we learned earlier, when anything presents itself to you, stop and define it at its most basic. Do not add value judgments. If you are about to partake in something you know goes against your best interest, strip that thing into its component parts. Clear away its mystique so you can move forward with a clear head.

What Is So Unbearable About This Moment?

> *"Don't panic before the picture of your entire life. Don't dwell on all the troubles you've faced or have yet to face, but instead ask yourself as each trouble comes, 'what is so unbearable or unmanageable in this?' Your reply will embarrass you. Then remind yourself that it's not the future or the past that bears down on you, but only the present. Always the present, which becomes an even smaller thing when isolated in this way and when the mind that cannot bear up under so slender an object is chastened."*

> —Marcus Aurelius, *Meditations* 8:36

A lot of the emotional weight of an event comes from your imagination. Physical sickness, grief, anxiety, all of these things can feel like they'll never go away. "I'll always feel like this," you might tell yourself. This isn't true, but it can feel true. Marcus Aurelius told himself to limit his troubles to the present. He looked at the very moment he was in and asked, "Is this truly unbearable? Is this moment the one that will break me?" The answer was always no. Here and now represents such a small moment compared to the huge, unknowable future. You can do the same. Whenever you are overwhelmed, circle the present and examine the moment. What is hard about this minute? Can you make it through the present and take one more step forward? Yes, you can.

Rate Your Emotions

Which negative states of mind do you most need to work on? On a scale of 1–5, 1 being a very healthy emotional life and 5 being a mind overwhelmed by that passion, rate yourself.

Fear _____

Appetite _____

Pleasure _____

Distress _____

NEGATIVE VISUALIZATION

> *"It is precisely in times of security that the soul should toughen itself beforehand for occasions of greater stress, and it is while Fortune is kind that it should fortify itself against her violence. In days of peace the soldier performs maneuvers, throws up earthworks with no enemy in sight, and wearies himself by gratuitous toil, in order that he may be equal to unavoidable toil. If you would not have a man flinch when the crisis comes, train him before it comes. Such is the course which those men have followed who, in their imitation of poverty, have every month come almost to want, that they might never recoil from what they had so often rehearsed."*

—Seneca, *Letters* 18

The Stoics believed you should rehearse the big challenges of life. They used both visualization techniques and physical practices to prepare themselves for the inevitable changes to come, in the hope that when the real challenge arrived, they would continue living in harmony. What are the challenges that would shake you? A terminal illness? A loved one dying? You already understand that, to the Stoic, these things are indifferent, in that they can't shake your virtue. Still, the Stoics were human and knew that such events strike at the core self. Therefore, they developed a habit of mentally walking themselves through the "worst" of challenges, so they could practice a Stoic outlook and wrestle with any improper value judgments that arose.

Mentally rehearsing big challenges is called "negative visualization." You might also see it called premeditation of adversity or, as I've already referred to it, premeditation of challenges. The idea is to visualize worst-case scenarios. Imagine a huge challenge as though it is happening. Then apply your tools, the Dichotomy of Control, the disciplines, and a focus on virtue, to train yourself to remain Stoic during the challenge.

- **What is in your control?**

- **What should you desire and avoid?**

- **Do you give in to the value judgments that bubble up, or do you reject them?**

- **How should you act?**

- **Can you remain in harmony, even during this? How?**

- **Can you even find joy in the moment, despite living what others would consider a catastrophe?**

These exercises help bring peace, both in the moment and also in the future when the big challenges arrive. Seneca tells us that expected events come as less of a shock. Negative visualizations can, at the least, help immunize you against the future. The greater hope is that these practices can stabilize your Stoic thinking so that when the challenge comes, it doesn't just dull the blow, but you continue to thrive as you meet the challenge head-on. Create a list of the hardest challenges you can imagine, the kind that would shake your world. Using the above guidelines and questions, begin to practice negative visualization on a regular basis. I will also share two variants on the practice that you can use.

Accepting Less

Seneca urged Stoics to take time to deprive themselves of the finer things. As a rich and influential Roman, this practice was meant to remind him that possessions are indifferents and, if they were taken from him, he should remain content. For a few days, or a week at a time, Seneca would stay in a barely furnished room, lay on a hard mat, eat bland, basic foods, and meditate on whether the good life came from external things or from himself.

You can adapt these practices to your own life. What can you let go of for a while that would help you see your virtuous self as independent from your possessions? You could eat the same, basic meal every day for a week. Many Stoics use cold showers as a way to accept discomfort as an indifferent. You could quit TV or the internet for a few days. Whatever you choose, remember to not just do the practice, but to engage your mind in a Stoic interrogation of your responses:

- **What is in your control?**

- **What should you desire and avoid?**

- **Do you assent to the value judgments that bubble up, or do you reject them?**

- **How should you act?**

- **Can you remain in harmony?**

- **Can you find joy in the moment, despite deprivation?**

I Knew I Was Mortal

When you read the Stoics, you'll find that death comes up a lot. After all, no one can escape death. The Stoics felt that coming to terms with that fact was essential for the philosopher, otherwise the fear of death would turn many of our actions away from wisdom. Socrates and Cato, both held up as Stoic heroes, chose to die rather than live a less virtuous life. Epictetus tells us that whenever a general paraded through Rome, slaves accompanied, their task to continuously whisper reminders of mortality into the general's ears. This was meant to humble him. For you, the negative visualization of your own death can help you accept that life itself is an indifferent.

Epictetus recommends you say, "I knew I was mortal," as you contemplate your death. In his *Discourses*, 3.24, he says that you should not be surprised by death because it is inevitable. Death is also not up to you; it is outside your control—an indifferent. As part of nature's harmony, we should accept death as a given. Using these thoughts, tell yourself, "Today is my last day." Think about death as inevitable, outside of your control, and natural. How then, should you respond to death when it comes?

A healthy mental life can help you act well in the world. As you find emotional freedom through your Stoic tools, you will find the Courage to seek out Justice wherever you can. In the next chapter, you will use your positive attitudes to take powerful actions for yourself, your community, and the world at large.

CHAPTER 7:
Being of Service

"At dawn, when you have trouble getting out of bed, tell yourself: 'I have to go to work — as a human being. What do I have to complain of, if I'm going to do what I was born for — the things I was brought into the world to do? Or is this what I was created for? To huddle under the blankets and stay warm?'"

—Marcus Aurelius, *Meditations* 5:1

Humans, in the Stoic view, are naturally social, meant to engage in healthy relationships with others. The Discipline of Action best represents this view. As you have already seen, your actions need to be focused on the community. As you focus on that which you can control, you still choose a path that benefits everyone, not only yourself. Your morning orientation reminds you that people will often be obstacles, but you can do your best to help them anyway. You are meant to live a life of service to your community. We're going to focus on being Stoic within relationships. Whether family, friends, or strangers, you will work to take actions that benefit them and you, using virtue as your guide.

How Stoics Treat Others

> *"Whatever then, we shall discover to be at the same time affectionate and consistent with reason, this we confidently declare to be right and good."*

—Epictetus, *Discourses* 1:11

Stoicism is a philosophy of love. The Stoic philosophers not only spoke of their love of wisdom, but also of their philanthropy, which means love of people. The Stoic theory of ethical development, called *oikeiosis*, expects you to grow in your ability to love until you have affection for the whole world. *Oikeiosis* is a complex idea, but in short, it says that all animals are born loving and preserving themselves. The social animals, humans included, expand that love first to immediate caregivers, then extended family, and, if we develop properly, we learn to have concern for all of humanity. The Stoic Hierocles described this growth using a series of concentric circles. The first circle of affection is yourself. The next is immediate family, followed by extended family and friends. After this comes your community, then surrounding communities, your country, and the whole of humankind. We modern Stoics tend to extend the circles outside of humanity as well, to truly encompass the world and all of its living creatures. Hierocles tells us that our task is to draw the outer circles closer to ourselves. He asks you to intentionally open yourself up to others and draw them close. The Stoic embraces the world.

Of course, no matter how much affection you show the world, you know that it doesn't always reciprocate. Stoicism is not naive in its acceptance of others. Recall the good passions. You will Wish the best for others, but you have Caution as protection when people exhibit less than their best behavior. A great example of this Caution is in *Meditations* 6:20, in which Marcus Aurelius uses the example of a wrestling match:

"In the ring our opponents can gouge us with their nails or butt us with their heads and leave a bruise, but we don't denounce them for it or get upset with them or regard them from then on as violent types. We just keep an eye on them after that. Not out of hatred or suspicion, just keeping a friendly distance. We need to do that in other areas. We need to excuse what our sparring partners do, and just keep our distance—without suspicion or hatred."

When people act out of ignorance, they take incorrect actions. In fact, Stoicism claims that all wrong actions stem from ignorance of a better way. You are asked to accept this about others because it is the human condition. However, you can also keep a friendly distance. Giving a person the space to grow does not require you to remain in a dangerous position. This is important to remember. Stoic resilience, and the healthy mind that comes with it, can free you. You can move past hurt, resentment, and fear and gain a willingness to love and accept others. Still, situations exist where Wisdom demands we walk away. Courage can help us overcome hard challenges, but Courage can also allow you to leave situations that are overwhelming.

Whenever you're faced with a challenging person, try to recall the following thoughts from *Meditations* 7:26, in which Marcus Aurelius says:

"When people injure you, ask yourself what good or harm they thought would come of it. If you understand that, you'll feel sympathy rather than outrage or anger. Your sense of good and evil may be the same as theirs, in which case you have to excuse them. Or your sense of good and evil may differ from theirs. In which case they're misguided and deserve your compassion. Is that so hard?"

It can be hard, but keeping your personal peace in the face of a difficult situation is also very rewarding. After all, why should you allow another person to take the harmony you've worked so hard to attain?

If They Knew All My Faults

> *"If you have been told that someone speaks ill of you, do not defend yourself: instead reply, 'if they knew the rest of my faults they wouldn't have mentioned only those.'"*

—Epictetus, *Enchiridion* 33

In relation to the other Stoic practices you've learned, self-deprecating humor might feel out of place. But the Stoics weren't against the use of humor, as long as you refrain from making fun of others. In this case, Epictetus recommends humor to control a potentially bad situation and as a form of humility. When someone talks about you behind your back, how do you respond? Many people would expect a defense along with a counterattack; neither response follows Stoic teachings. You defend yourself when attacked, but words said by another—particularly when out of earshot—fall into the indifferent category. Another person's opinion of you cannot tarnish your virtue. And you attacking another person's reputation equates to an unvirtuous act. Epictetus's suggestion: Defuse the situation by acknowledging that you have flaws and then move on to another topic.

It Seemed So to Them

> *"When any person treats you badly or speaks ill of you, remember that they do this because they think they must. It's not possible for them to do what you think is right, but only what seems right to them . . . if you understand this you will have a milder temper with those who revile you because you can always say, 'it seemed so to them.'"*

—Epictetus, *Enchiridion* 42

It seemed so to them helps you remain grounded and in harmony when a person becomes challenging. We'd all prefer to never be slandered or attacked, but confrontations happen. So how can you keep a good flow of life? By recognizing the other person's situation. They believe something that is wrong. Wrong beliefs lead to negative thoughts and actions—the passions. The only way out of that pattern is to change their beliefs, and you probably aren't in the position to teach this person right now. Tell yourself, "They are doing what they think is best." This way, you can leave behind any negative feelings about them and concentrate on the positive, virtuous actions that you are going to take in the moment.

To be clear: This practice does not absolve anyone of bad actions. Wrong is wrong. It's simply an acknowledgment that their unfounded beliefs make it impossible for them to do better in the moment. They remain accountable for how they behave.

FRIENDS AND FAMILY

> *"The wise are self-sufficient. Nevertheless, they desire friends, neighbors, and associates, no matter how much they are sufficient unto themselves."*

—Seneca, *Letters from a Stoic* 9

Close relationships are meant to be comforting and to bring out the best in you. This is not always the case. As the saying goes, you can't choose your family! Even your associates are often imposed on you, a consequence of where you live or work. This can tax your energy and create situations that require every tool in your Stoic tool kit. And yet Stoicism asks you to remain virtuous throughout it all, to be your best self whether or not everyone else repays the favor. How can you do this?

In *Discourses* 3:28, Epictetus talks with a student who is having difficulties with his father. He tells him that, "Your father has a certain function, and if he does not perform it, he has destroyed the father in him, the man who loves his offspring, the man of gentleness within him. Do not seek to make him lose anything else on this account. For it never happens that a man goes wrong in one thing, but is injured in another. Again, it is your function to defend yourself firmly, respectfully, without passion. Otherwise, you have destroyed within you the son, the respectful man, the man of honor."

Here, you see a common Stoic viewpoint. In a relationship, each person has a role to play. The Stoic, of course, only controls his own role. Epictetus says that the father's actions are of no consequence to the Stoic student, the relationship is an indifferent. The student is asked to focus his attention on his own thoughts and actions, rather than dwell on his father's choices. He's asked to never engage the bad passions, to be certain to not become disrespectful. He's also told to defend himself firmly. Here again, Stoicism does not leave you passive. It is always appropriate to stand up for yourself, as long as you do so with virtue in mind. The Dichotomy of Control, when applied to relationships, is not meant to lead you to invest less in others, but to invest in yourself more wisely. You can't control others, and their actions should not control you. If you focus on what is yours—your opinions, impulses, and desires—you will make proper value judgments, take meaningful actions, and be your best self in every relationship. Often, this will help your relationships become healthy and joyful. Sometimes your best will not be reciprocated, but you will know that you tried and have the ability to continue on in harmony no matter the outcome.

What do the disciplines tell you about relationships? The Discipline of Desire reminds you not to long for or fear particular actions from the people you know. Instead, you want to be your best in the relationship, and only fear that you might treat others poorly. The Discipline of Assent gives you mental tools so you don't jump to bad conclusions concerning other people's actions. Did someone just say something mean? No need to judge them, just choose how best to respond. The

Discipline of Action focuses your choices on what will benefit both of you. This protects you from taking actions at the other person's expense.

Stoicism Applied to Social Life

In this exercise, match the situation with a Stoic technique that can protect or return you to harmony.

A friend seems upset and you can't help but think that they are angry at you.	A. Amor Fati
A parent keeps saying embarrassing things, and you feel that this reflects poorly on you.	B. Circle the Present
You are on a date and keep getting distracted by thoughts of possible future dates.	C. You Are Just an Appearance
Your friends have been visiting from out of town; it has been a great time, but they leave tomorrow.	D. Circle Yourself

Answer key page 165

IN THE MOMENT

Epictetus says that within a troublesome relationship you should avoid passions, remain respectful, and defend yourself appropriately. Bring to mind a difficult relationship from your past or present. Review your own actions:

- How would you have handled the relationship if you had been practicing Stoicism?

- How can you prepare yourself for similar situations in the future?

LIVING IN SOCIETY

> *"Let us take hold of the fact that there are two communities—the one, which is great and truly common, embracing gods and humans, in which we look neither to this corner nor that, but measure the boundaries of our citizenship by the sun; the other, the one to which we were assigned by the accident of our birth."*
>
> —Seneca, *On Leisure*

Stoicism brings the best out of you so that you can give your best to the world around you. So many challenges—small and large—could benefit from the contribution of wise and courageous people just like you. Of course, in an ideal world, stepping up to help meant that everyone would accept that help and join in, but community is a messy thing. People work at cross-purposes. So how do you tackle that as a Stoic?

> *". . . we were born into this world to work together like the feet, hands, eyelids, or upper and lower rows of teeth."*
>
> —Marcus Aurelius, *Meditations* 2:1

Stoicism views all people as part of a single organism, or one big human family. This imagery is everywhere in Stoic writing. In *Discourses* 2:10, Epictetus says, "What then does the character of a citizen promise? To hold nothing as profitable to himself; to deliberate about nothing as if we were detached from the community, but to act as the hand or foot would do, if they had reason and understood the constitution of nature, for they would never put themselves in motion nor desire anything, otherwise than with reference to the whole."

Here you see that the human connection matters so much that every action requires taking others' best interest into account, not just our own. This rounds out the perspective you already learned from the Discipline of Action. It can also inform the practices you learned with that discipline. Marcus Aurelius's morning orientation ends with these lines, "To obstruct each other is unnatural. To feel anger at someone, to turn your back on him: these are unnatural." As you begin your day, remember that you want to be prepared to accept the less-than-perfect people you will meet, but you also should be willing to assist them if the occasion arises. You can apply the two missions practice as well. You want to do x, but you also want to keep in harmony with life. Stoic harmony indeed fosters internal contentment, but also encourages active, virtuous engagement with the world. Understanding this helps keep you focused on the virtuous path.

Of course, not all engagement with society requires a hard struggle. For example, I like to volunteer at our local farmers' market. My family heads down every Sunday as the market closes and helps take down the stalls and other equipment. We do this because we value what the market brings to our neighborhood, both in terms of healthy food and the social impact of a place where neighbors interact with one another. Stoicism encourages you to invest time and effort in your community.

What moves you? What do you value in your neighborhood or what would you like to see more of? People already doing that work would likely welcome your contribution. If no one is yet doing the work, maybe you can start something. Whatever the case, as your practice improves your courage, your sense of justice, and your willingness to work with others, take initiative and put your ideas into action.

IN THE MOMENT

"I will show the nerves of a philosopher. 'What nerves are these?' A desire never disappointed, an aversion which never falls on that which it would avoid, a proper pursuit, a diligent purpose, an assent which is not rash. These you shall see."

—EPICTETUS, *DISCOURSES* 2:8

As sketched out in this quote, Stoicism is meant to make you strong. As you practice the philosophy, return to this line. Are you showing the nerves of a philosopher?

REFLECTIONS

"Let your impulse to act and your action have as their goal the service of the human community, because that, for you, is in conformity with your nature."

—MARCUS AURELIUS, *MEDITATIONS* 9:31

Serving your community is healthy. It can help you feel engaged with a world that can often seem distant and overwhelming. In particular, acting at a local level can help you when larger issues feel completely outside your grasp. If you ever feel individually helpless in relation to a larger world problem or particular event, there is a way to overcome that state of mind. First, use the Dichotomy of Control and similar practices to focus yourself on what you control. When it comes to world events, you'll find that all news lies outside of your control. However, that does not leave you passive.

- What is it about this event that concerns you? Does it affect your sense of justice, for instance?

- Is there a similar issue in your own community?

- **If so, are there people who are working to address this issue?**

- **What virtuous actions can you take to address the issue in your own life, in your own community?**

CAN STOICS CREATE CHANGE?

The Roman Stoics had a hero named Cato, a statesman who devoted himself to the Stoic path. Later Stoics held him up as exemplary for multiple reasons. He was known by all to have deep moral integrity and to be immune to bribes. He remained uncompromising in his values, earning the respect even of his political enemies. Most of all, the Stoics admired him because he chose to die rather than yield when his side was defeated in a civil war. This was proof that he valued virtue even more than the preferred indifferent known as life.

The Stoic heroes were all people who worked to overcome challenges. The mythic Hercules faced tremendous trials. Socrates challenged his society, which, like Cato, led to his death. Diogenes lived a life of confrontation, directly challenging the social values of his day. Stoics consider these people exemplary. It's obvious, then, that virtuous people are expected both to face challenges when they come and to push through resistance, if that is what virtue requires.

> *"When you do a thing because you have determined that it ought to be done, never avoid being seen doing it, even if the opinion of the multitude is going to condemn you. For if your action is wrong, then avoid doing it altogether, but if it is right, why do you fear those who will rebuke you wrongly?"*

—Epictetus, *Enchiridion* 35

Stoic courage is meant to make you active. Stoic control is meant to make you focused. Stoic indifference never leads to apathy; it develops fearlessness. You're free to pursue excellence with all the energy you can muster, when you are no longer weighed down by anxiety concerning indifferents. The Stoic mind-set makes you an activist, in whatever way that applies to your life.

As you choose how to work with your community, remember to focus on what you control rather than the possible outcomes of any one project. In "Letters from a Stoic 14," Seneca says, "The wise person looks to the purpose of all actions, not their consequences; beginnings are in our power but Fortune judges the outcome." Cato lost his war but is considered a hero because he stood for justice. In a similar way, your success is decided by the actions you take and the reasons you took them; you cannot guarantee a desired outcome.

The topics we've just covered can take a lifetime to perfect. You have relationships old and new to navigate. Your community's needs will change, and the communities you are a part of will likely change as well. Once you've finished this book, what will be your next steps? In the final chapter I'll give suggestions for continued practice and for additional reading, starting with the ancient Stoics themselves. You'll be left with plenty of options as you go forth on your Stoic journey.

CHAPTER 8:
Continuing Your Journey

> *"Why all this guesswork? You can see what needs to be done. If you can see the road, follow it. Cheerfully, without turning back. If not, hold up and get the best advice that you can. If anything gets in the way, forge on ahead, making good use of what you have on hand, sticking to what seems right."*

> —Marcus Aurelius, *Meditations* 10:12

You *can* thrive in this life. The tools from this book are yours to use and, when you wield them consistently, you can break through obstacles and capture joy. In this final chapter, I'll recommend next steps in your practice, and I'll set you loose on the old Stoics themselves, so you can learn from them directly. These new resources can enrich your Stoic journey, but you already have what you need. Intentional and constant practice helps you achieve the biggest gains—the good flow of life.

Consistent Stoic Practice

> *"Could someone acquire instant self-control by merely knowing that they must not be con-quered by pleasures but without training to resist them? Could someone become just by learning that they must love moderation but without practicing the avoidance of excess? Could we acquire courage by realizing that things which seem terrible to most people are not to be feared but without practicing being fearless towards them?"*
>
> —Musonius Rufus, from the lecture on practicing philosophy

You will continue to unlock the benefits of Stoicism through practice. As you train yourself to recall Stoic phrases like, "You are just an appearance" or "It was returned," you'll find they come to mind more quickly and arrive at opportune moments. You'll train yourself to naturally express the lessons you've learned through the disciplines. Having these tools at the ready will protect your harmony. The ups and downs of life will appear more even because you can overcome the challenges you face. To change your life for the better, you can't leave practice to chance. You can't simply hope you'll recall things in the hard moments. You need a plan. To assist you on your journey, I recommend three things: memorization, journaling, and developing a daily routine.

COMMIT IT TO MEMORY

You need your Stoic tools at a moment's notice, and they only work if you can recall them. Starting with the practices, techniques, or outlooks that have impacted you so far, memorize a quote or phrase that helps you bring them to mind. One of my favorites is "festival." That simple word reminds me of the Stoic love of people, my need to let go, and so much more. I cannot count the number of times that I felt better by quickly remembering and then saying, "festival" under my breath.

Make Stoicism part of your mental life by working to embed it into your thoughts.

JOURNAL

If you want to keep progressing in the philosophy, write. Journaling remains a key component of Stoic practice. The book we know as *Meditations* was a personal journal that the emperor Marcus Aurelius kept to meditate on philosophy and wrestle with his flaws. He grew through that practice. He could compare who he was to who he aspired to be. I started my website, *Immoderate Stoic*, as a public journal 10 years ago, and I still sometimes go through past posts to see who I was then and to compare with who I am now. This same practice will benefit you. Choose a way to converse with yourself. Paper and pen, a notes app on your phone, a blog—just find a consistent way to record your thoughts.

ESTABLISH A DAILY ROUTINE

Finally, choose a few practices to integrate into your daily life. For instance, you can start the day with the morning orientation and end it with the evening reflection. Creating a Stoic routine is grounding. It will help strengthen your impromptu use of the tools because your mind will already be centered in a Stoic outlook. After choosing one or two things to practice daily, I suggest picking other techniques to practice at different intervals. Perhaps every Sunday morning you set aside time to meditate on the view from above, or set aside time to practice a particularly impactful negative visualization. Creating a Stoic pattern will help you cultivate the harmony that you seek.

REFLECTION

"Never call yourself a philosopher, or talk a great deal about your principles to the multitude, but act on your principles. For instance, at an entertainment, don't talk about how people ought to eat, but eat as you ought."

—EPICTETUS, *ENCHIRIDION* 46

In a number of places, Epictetus reminded his students to live the life of philosophy instead of talking about it. He warned them against telling others about changes they should make, without making those changes in themselves. As you integrate Stoicism into your life, you may be tempted to overshare with others. Before doing so, ask yourself a few questions and remind yourself of the Stoic outlook.

- Am I acting as a Stoic right now, or am I only talking about Stoicism?

- Have I actually been asked for advice in this situation? Unsolicited advice is rarely accepted and can be counterproductive.

- Stoicism is about a harmonious life. How can I show the life of a Stoic without words?

Extremes

Consistent practice pays off when especially hard challenges come your way. The Stoic ideal is to meet every moment in the same way—positive and resilient—while remaining in harmony with the world. But when faced with a true challenge (whether a result of who you are as an individual or just because you are human), your best hope is to have already prepared through diligent practice. We've discussed how negative visualization can help in these moments. Along with that practice, I find that recalling the Stoic short phrases as well as using the view from above can be particularly helpful in stressful times.

Challenging events often stay with us for a while; they don't just hit us in the moment. You might be having a pleasant day when a stray thought suddenly brings something back. This calls for a strategic, "You are just an appearance and not the thing you claim to be" mantra. "This is nothing to me" can also serve you well. In moments when you don't have the freedom to walk off and meditate on a Stoic outlook, these quick and effective practices can help snap you back into a better mental space. When I first started practicing Stoicism in earnest, I wrote a few phrases onto a piece of paper that I carried in my pocket. Whenever I felt stress rising, I unfolded that page and picked whatever phrase I needed to center myself. Find a method that works for you and stick to it.

ZOOMING OUT HELPS

Peace can also be maintained by viewing your present troubles in light of the entire world. The view from above is meant to expand your consciousness beyond the personal toward a more universal mind-set. This practice can take overwhelming thoughts and place them into a more manageable context. In *Meditations* 9:30, Marcus Aurelius says, "Look down from above on the countless herds of men and their countless solemnities, and the infinitely varied voyagings in storms and calms, and the differences among those who are born, who live together, and die. And consider, too, the life lived by others in olden time, and the life of those who will live after thee, and the life now lived among barbarous nations, and how many know not even thy name, and how many will soon forget it, and how they who perhaps now are praising thee will very soon blame thee, and that neither a posthumous name is of any value, nor reputation, nor anything else." Thoughts like these can remind you how very grounded in the human experience your present challenge really is. In those moments where it is particularly hard to separate what you control from the rest, where your desires are still very much focused on indifferents, taking the time to mentally step back and rest can provide enough space to regain your footing.

You are striving to be your best. There are times that will challenge that. In *Discourses* 3:25, Epictetus says, "In this contest, even if we should falter for a while, no one can prevent us from resuming the fight, nor is it necessary to wait another four years for the next Olympic Games to come around, but as soon as one has recovered and regained one's strength, and can muster the same zeal as before, one can enter the fight; and if one should fail again, one can enter once again, and if one should carry off the victory one fine day, it will be as if one had never given in." Always remember that you can try again. If you stumble in the moment, get up, refresh yourself, and start moving forward.

GOOD FORTUNE

Good times are also a place for Stoic thinking. As we've already seen, the gifts of Fortune are great, but they are not guaranteed. Enjoying the good things without thinking about their impermanence will leave you vulnerable to a hard fall when change comes. Avoiding this doesn't mean denying yourself pleasure or holding back your commitment to life in an effort to protect yourself. No. You should fully embrace these gifts. You do this by paying true attention to the moment while realizing that change is going to come.

How many people have expressed regret at not appreciating what they had when they had it? Your Stoic outlook will help you invest in the things that you have, saving you from ever feeling that you missed the good times. Circling the present is an essential part of loving your life. When you're with a person that you care for, draw your attention to them, to the moment you are sharing. Don't allow your thoughts to be lost in desires or fears of the future. At the same time, don't forget that everything you have is on loan. Someday you will return it. This makes the present moment all the more important. Why waste your time on the unknowable future when you can find happiness in the present moment? Invest fully in the now so that when change comes, there will be no sense of loss, because you truly got all you could from the time that you had.

To paraphrase Marcus Aurelius, if you deal with bad times properly, they'll actually become good times. With that in mind, meditate on how the events are indifferent, and how you can thrive all the time.

- **What do "bad times" mean to a Stoic?**

- **What does a "good time" mean in our philosophy?**

- **What benefits are there to embracing the Stoic view of events?**

- **How can this viewpoint help you maintain a harmonious life?**

True or False?

Negative visualization is meant to prepare you for the hard challenges of life. In the following list, decide if each statement about negative visualization is true or false.

- **You should visualize a difficulty as if it is happening to you right now. _____**

- **Negative visualization helps you worry now, so that later you worry less. _____**

- **Negative visualization helps you understand indifferents and that events, in themselves, are neither good nor bad. _____**

- **You should only visualize small challenges—events such as breakups, house fires, and death are too much to handle. _____**

- **Negative visualization can help you realize that change is necessary, natural, and to be expected. _____**

- **Negative visualization is meant to make you into a pessimist. _____**

Answer key page 165

- Negative visualization can help cultivate good passions and lead you to a better understanding of Amor Fati. _____

IN THE MOMENT

Many Stoics recall their practices in the hard times but forget to apply them on easy days. Think back through the many Stoic practices and decide which would help you during the good times:

Which mind-sets will cultivate good passions, and which will help you keep those good passions even when new challenges arise?

Sustained Happiness

I began this book with a quote from Marcus Aurelius, "Waste no more time thinking about what a good person should be, just be one." You have what you need to transform into the best version of you. That's really the point of Stoicism: to impress upon you that happiness is within your grasp—if you know how to get it. As you go out and apply Stoicism to your life, pay attention to how it affects you. Are you developing more Wisdom, Courage, Moderation, and Justice in your life? Are you finding more moments of Joy? Seneca tells us, "No school has more goodness and gentleness; none has more love for human beings, nor more attention to the common good. The goal which it assigns to us is to be useful, to help others, and to take care, not only of ourselves, but of everyone in general and of each one in particular." Do you find yourself expressing these qualities? If so, you are on a path of harmony and you've developed a good flow of life.

One of the best ways to grow in your philosophy is to become part of a Stoic community. The most accessible way to do this is to seek out online Stoic forums. There are groups on all the major social media platforms from which you can gain insights, ask for help, and just talk with others who are walking the same path as you. It is also possible that there are local face-to-face Stoic groups in your area. A website called The Stoic Fellowship collects the details of a variety of Stoic meetups that happen across the world. There is also a helpful guide to starting a group if there isn't one in your area. Stoic groups have the same diversity of thought that any other assembly of people would include, so understand that you might have to practice your Stoicism to get along with fellow Stoics, but there is a lot of value in having real people to talk to about your journey.

"Not to feel exasperated, or defeated, or despondent because your days aren't packed with wise and moral actions. But to get back up when you fail, to celebrate behaving like a human—however imperfectly—and fully embrace the pursuit you've embarked on."

—Marcus Aurelius, *Meditations* 5:9

Thinking back on your personal values, what will motivate you to continue on after a failure? What changes in your life will be the biggest signs of progress? Which exercises can you practice that have the greatest chance of bringing about that personal progress?

Stoicism has given you tools, but you are the one who will use them to overcome challenges to become your best self. You have all that you need to lead a flourishing life. Go out and show your resilience, find your joy, and use your uniqueness to create a better world.

RESOURCES

The Canon

We have precious few writings from the ancient Stoics, but what we do have is very much worth getting to know. Most of these texts have many editions, translations, and the like. The beauty of the modern age is that many are also available freely on the internet as well.

I suggest that you first read the *Enchiridion*. The *Enchiridion*, or handbook, is a collection of Epictetus's sayings compiled by one of his students. It's a bit like a study guide to Stoic philosophy, although it's definitely not comprehensive. The *Enchiridion* will give you many things to think about.

Next, find yourself a copy of *Meditations* by Marcus Aurelius. This journal is a glimpse into the mind of a practicing Stoic, and I find this philosopher to feel more like a companion than a teacher. The *Meditations* was not meant to be published, so you will notice that the writing is often haphazard. The emperor's life rarely followed a theme; it just happened and he wrote about it. Still, within its 12 books, there are so many lessons that speak to life today, no matter the distance between us and Marcus Aurelius in both time and social position.

I suggest, on your first read, that you start at book 2. Book 1 often comes off as dry and doesn't really reflect the tone of the whole journal.

Seneca wrote so much, and we have access to a lot of it. I suggest you first read his *Letters from a Stoic*. This book compiles 124 letters that Seneca wrote near the end of his life. They cover a wide range of subjects that highlight the Stoic view of life, death, and all those topics in between.

Those three books will serve you for quite a while. In my case, I've been reading the *Meditations* and the *Enchiridion* consistently for a decade. However, if you want more of the old writings, I would suggest picking up Musonius Rufus's *Lectures and Sayings*, as well as a copy of Epictetus's *Discourses*. Musonius was Epictetus's teacher, and the few words we have from him really show what the Stoic school was all about. The Discourses expand on the lessons of the *Enchiridion*. You'll gain a much richer understanding of the thinking behind Stoicism and how it is meant to be applied.

The website Modern Stoicism will provide you with Stoic articles from a variety of perspectives. It is an invaluable resource and a great starting point as you reach out to a wider world of Stoic practitioners. You can also find information on Stoic Week, which provides a wonderful opportunity to put your knowledge into practice.

REFERENCES

Aurelius, Marcus. *Meditations*. Translated by Gregory Hays. London: Phoenix, 2003.

Epictetus. *The Discourses of Epictetus; with the Enchiridion and Fragments*. Translated by George Long. London: George Bell and Sons, 1800.

Hadot, Pierre. *The Inner Citadel: The Meditations of Marcus Aurelius*. Cambridge: Harvard University Press, 1998.

Rufus, Musonius. *Lectures & Sayings*. Translated by Cynthia King. CreateSpace, 2011.

Seneca. *Letters from a Stoic*. Translated by Robin Campbell. London: Penguin Group, 1973.

Seneca. *Moral Essays Volume I*. Translated by John Basore. Cambridge: Harvard University Press, 1928.

Seneca. *Moral Essays Volume II*. Translated by John Basore. Cambridge: Harvard University Press, 1932.

INDEX

ACKNOWLEDGMENTS

My Stoicism has been shaped by a wide range of people—some of whom I've met and many of whom have affected me from afar. I owe a particular debt to the organization Modern Stoicism. Their website and books have provided a wealth of perspective from fellow modern Stoics. I am also grateful to both Patrick Ussher and Gregory Sadler for inviting me to publish through their site. Many of their team, in particular Donald Robertson, Chris Gill, John Sellars, and Massimo Pigliucci, have also influenced my understanding and practice.

Mark Johnston and Greg Milner helped me find a voice through the podcast *Painted Porch*. Stoics in Action and the companion Stoics for Justice Facebook page have kept me hopeful for the development of our philosophy in the modern world. The many listeners of my podcast, *Good Fortune*, continue to ask me hard questions and keep me honest.

I also love my neighborhood of Montavilla. Without Townshend's Teahouse, Bipartisan Cafe, and Beer Bunker, this book would not have been written.

ABOUT THE AUTHOR

 **Matthew J. Van Natta** is the creator of the Stoic podcast *Good Fortune* and the blog Immoderate Stoic. His writings focus on the daily application of Stoicism in the modern world. He lives with his wife and daughter in Portland, Oregon.

ANSWER KEY

Page 31: C, F, D, B, A, E
Page 134: C, D, B, A
Page 153: True, False, True, False, True, False, True